Reimagining Adoption

WHAT ADOPTEES SEEK
from FAMILIES and FAITH

Sally Ankerfelt, M. Div.

Gayle H. Swift, CPC

Braided Threads Publishing
Palm City, Florida

Copyright © 2019 by Sally Ankerfelt, M.Div., Gayle H. Swift, CPC.
Cover image: fotolia

All rights reserved. No part of this publication may be reproduced, distributed or transmitted in any form or by any means, including photocopying, recording, or other electronic or mechanical methods, without the prior written permission of the publisher, except in the case of brief quotations embodied in critical reviews and certain other noncommercial uses permitted by copyright law. For permission requests, write to the publisher, addressed "Attention: Permissions Coordinator," at the address below.

Braided Threads Publishing /Sally Ankerfelt, Gayle H. Swift
2285 SW Olympic Club Terrace
Palm City, Florida 34990
www.gaylehswift.com

Book Layout ©2017 BookDesignTemplates.com

Ordering Information:
Quantity sales. Special discounts are available on quantity purchases by corporations, associations, and others. For details, contact the "Special Sales Department" at the address above.

Reimagining Adoption: What Adoptees Seek from Families and Faith, Sally Ankerfelt, M.Div., Gayle H. Swift, CPC.
—1st ed.
ISBN: 978-1-7336597-2-7

Table of Contents

Find the Grace of Open Hearts and Minds 5

1: Act of Faith: Adoption-attunement 8

2: General Cultural Beliefs that Influence Adoption in America 21

3: Cultural Belief: That Adoptees Do Not Need To Know about Their Birth Families 46

4: Scriptural Interpretation Supported the Fracture of Families 59

5: Scripture: Adoptees Heard a Message of Exclusion 80

6: Listen, Learn, and Lean in with Empathy 94

7: What Parents and Families Can Do 114

8: Rethink God's Will as a Justification for Adoption 126

9: The Power of Words: Language Matters 142

10: Acknowledge and Address Racism and White Privilege in The Church 166

11: How We Can Help When Trauma Comes to Church 183

Conclusion 195

Acknowledgments 198

Appendix 200

Elements of Adoption-attunement 217

Additional Resources 220

Websites 221

Suggested Reading for Adults 227

Suggested Reading for Children 230

Bibliography 231

Index 235

About the Authors 243

Titles Available for children 244

Testimonials 246

Dedication

To all who have been touched by adoption, especially my beloved children and their first families, and to those adoptees and first parents who had the courage to share from their hearts. —GHS

To all the children around the world, to those who gave of themselves by answering our survey: adoptees, first parents and adoptive parents; to my husband and my children whom I love and cherish, and to The Church who is called to bring the love of Christ to the world. —SASA

PREFACE

Find the Grace of Open Hearts and Minds

A mere two miles from the congregation Sally serves in Minneapolis, you can find the office of the Seward Longfellow Restorative Justice Partnership. They coordinate conferences between crime victims, offenders, and any community member impacted by the crime. Their goal is "to build community by providing the opportunity to repair harm by involving the victim, offender, and community in solutions that promote healing, accountability, and reconciliation."[1]

---

[1] https://sng.org/restorativejustice/

Dr. Mark Umbreit, founding director of the Center for Restorative Justice and Peacemaking at the University of Minnesota, believes that respect, openness, and compassion are the underlying components of engagement. He reflects, "Restorative dialogue is one of many pathways to a deeper experience of forgiveness. It's about creating a safe space to go deep within your heart, to feel vulnerability, to be open to others' pain, to recognize their humanity at the deepest level."[2]

This book serves as a virtual conference. We recall the history and some current practices surrounding adoption, not to shame, but to listen, learn, love, and be the responsive church we are called to be. Much of what you will read in this section did not personally involve us or you the reader. But, as the Body of Christ today, we choose to gather with adoptees and their families in Christian community. We choose to hear how The Church and society, despite good intentions, followed some practices and policies which caused some unintended, painful consequences for many adoptees and their families. They ask us to witness the pain The Church has inflicted and, on behalf of The Church, to accept responsibility for its actions. Love is essential but love alone is not enough. Repentance, forgiveness, and accountability are also essential. When we choose this path, we can pave the way for repair and reconciliation.

The blessing of forgiveness is deeply rooted in Christian ethos. Jesus taught us, "Forgive us our trespasses as we

---

[2] https://charterforcompassion.org/forgiveness-and-reconciliation

forgive those who trespass against us…" Those who have been wronged often say that the most painful barrier to healing and potential forgiveness is lack of accountability and responsibility by the transgressor. When we do not say, "I see how this hurt you," we block the way to a more loving and humane system. Wounds remain unhealed and relationships remain damaged.

On the other hand, when we choose to acknowledge the missteps of the past and take the opportunity to practice accountability, we implement a key element of the path to reconciliation. When we change our actions, we make way for the power of forgiveness to build a bridge from the past to the future, from the pain to the repair, from the violation to the restoration of the relationship. Our new actions will reflect the expansive love of Christ that we profess.

This book includes insights and strategies to reverse the unintended consequence of fractured spiritual relationships so that The Church and Christian families truly can become the embodiment of Christ's love for adoptees and their families.

CHAPTER 1

Act of Faith: Adoption-attunement

Since both The Church and society have accepted adoption as a preferred way to help vulnerable children, have you ever wondered how well adoptees have fared? Though we always hope that children will thrive in their adoptive families, statistics reveal that children who are separated from their family experience profound, life-long grief and loss. How can The Church meet the needs of these children and their families in ways that reflect Christian love and mitigate any harmful effects? This book represents our answer to that question.

As you read this book, you may experience surprise, sadness, and empathy just as we experienced when we first began our research and received input from adult adoptees. We did not realize that some of the actions and beliefs of The Church—however well-intended—have caused shame, pain, confusion, and loss of faith within the adoption community. The information may take some time for you to digest and ponder, just as it did for us. You may draw the same conclusion we did: we need to do things differently. Thankfully we believe in a God who sent Christ into the world to forgive sins and bring new life. As Christians, we have a process by which to seek forgiveness and move forward with a fresh start and new resolve: examine our collective conscience, acknowledge our actions, seek forgiveness, and resolve to act differently in the future. We want to do better and we *can* do better!

This book models a process of asking for forgiveness and the resolve to transform our new understanding into action. We begin with the historical, cultural, and scriptural background of adoption outside and inside The Church. We tell the truth and acknowledge wrongs that have been done by our American culture and The Church, whether intentional or not. The purpose of this truth-telling is not to cause pain, but to help heal. Then, we move forward with new understanding and action that, hopefully, will begin the process of healing for adoptees and first families as well as for The Church.

The Church's goal remains the same: to be a primary vehicle for adoptees and birth families to know that there is a place for them in this world and in the Body of Christ. We simply need a new way to do it.

Reimagining Adoption: What Adoptees Seek from Families and Faith aims to open hearts, minds, and eyes to the realities of adoption. It invites The Church—as congregations and as individual Christians—to reinvent their role in adoption and offers new ideas for ministry so that we, truly, can be part of Christ's healing.

The Church we love has the power to help people heal. It can help people reconnect with themselves, others, and Christ. This is not just a spiritual healing, but a body-mind healing, as well. We as The Church practice wellness through song, the telling of God's story, confession and forgiveness, prayer, and fellowship. We already have the tools to be a source of healing for those whose lives are fragmented. The challenge is for us to adapt these tools to meet the unique needs of people touched by adoption.

This book offers many practical and effective ways to reinvigorate and reshape the way Christians understand and approach adoption. The ideas it presents not only align with our faith but also respect and validate the genuine needs of adoptees, first families, and adoptive families.

What qualifies us to write this book? We are both certified coaches who specialize in providing support and resources to adoptees and their families. (We do not facilitate adoptions.) Sally is a Lutheran pastor. She and her husband, Dan, are adoptive parents to three children: one child adopted internationally, one through an open adoption, and one through the foster care system. Sally and Dan are white. Their children are people of color.

Gayle is an author. She adopted her two children as infants in the 1980's. Their placements were originally "closed." Both have reconnected with their first mothers with the help, encouragement, and support of Gayle and her husband, George. In addition to her coaching work, Gayle writes extensively on adoption issues.

Through our work at GIFT Family Services, we focus on how to serve adoptees and the families who love and support them. We wrote this book to offer more effective ways to be the living embodiment of Christ's love, light, and healing in ministry with adoptees and their families—birth and adoptive.

As adoptive parents we experienced how misunderstandings and lack of knowledge shaped the way people saw our families and how they responded to us and our needs. We love our children and it breaks our hearts to see how misinformation about adoption complexity can lead to lack of empathy. Not only sad, uninformed, and hurtful, such misinformation actually damages adoptees spiritually, physically, and psychologically.

We soon realized that although we had amassed hard-won knowledge and insight, we were not the true experts. Adoptees are. They are the ones *living* this experience. We had no place to speak on behalf of adoptees without their input. The most important voice of all—the adoptee voice—must be our central vantage point—not a peripheral perspective!

We needed to hear their stories. We consulted several adult adoptees. They, in turn, connected us with other adoptees who responded with passion. We received many heartfelt responses that revealed facts of adoptee life stories. They told us what had worked for them as well as how they yearned for things to be different in their faith communities and at home. Their stories touched our hearts and opened our minds.

We listened, pondered, and learned. We set aside our preconceived notions. As an act of respect, we listened without refutation. We were mindful of the words of theologian David Augsberger that being heard equates with feeling loved. We strove to represent every note, not just the lovely harmonies, but also the discordant, challenging ones.

With each group of the adoption circle who responded to our survey, we heard a common theme: They felt as if they did not belong. Unheard. Invalidated. Clearly these results were not what loving faith communities intended. We, as congregations, want to serve our members and seek to "love one another as Christ first loved us."

Our discussions in this book include many quotations from adult adoptees. We appreciate their courage and honesty and believe their words will fall on the "fertile soil" of our reader's hearts and minds. Of course, their voices will not represent the voices of all or the perspectives of all. No single narrative captures the story of all adoptees. Their words do reveal recurring themes that point to common experiences. These similarities have informed our reflections and conclusions.

Adoptees and first mothers shared poignant, personal, and often heartbreaking stories. While they were eager to speak with us, many respondents were reluctant to be identified publicly. Our intuition told us that this need for anonymity indicated something important. So, we raised this issue in some adoptee forums on Facebook. Their replies revealed that many factors had influenced their request even beyond the natural inclination to keep personal information private and to respect the privacy of their family members.

Personal experience has taught them it was unsafe to speak out. When they talk about the painful and challenging aspects of adoption, they frequently encounter pushback, criticism, dismissal, and anger. Such encounters are scary in addition to being unpleasant and invalidating. Fear heightens their reluctance to be identified—fear of blowback, fear of offending their families, fear of rejection, and fear of attack from an unreceptive audience.[3] They want to avoid ugly debates which condemn their story because it does not fit the listener's expectations. Such dramatic confrontations exhaust them and leave them feeling further traumatized. Anonymity provided a layer of protection that made them feel safe enough to speak their truth and trust that their insights will educate those willing to listen.

For those who have been shut down or dismissed, *Reimagining Adoption: What Adoptees Seek from Families and Faith* opens a space for them to have an experience of listening, non-judgmental ears. It provides an opportunity for The Church to offer support. The book stands on the belief that when we have the courage to discover ways in

---

[3] http://noapologiesforbeingme.blogspot.com/2015/11/what-we-gain-when-adoptees-tell-their.html

which we have missed the mark and are honest in our self-evaluation, we come closer to the vision God holds for us. We model the belief that truth-seeking is a holy and healing endeavor.

We believe that faith communities can and want to do a better job of supporting adoptees. Some communities are working to reflect this more compassionate understanding of adoption realities. However, when churches lack the appropriate education and understanding, their efforts can misfire and they can fall short of their desire to minister to those in their ranks who have been touched by adoption (adoptees, first parents, adoptive parents, and their extended families.)

Reimagining Adoption: What Adoptees Seek from Families and Faith shows how we as parents and communities of faith can serve adoptees and their families well. It helps adoptees and their families understand each other better and offers ways that they can ask for and receive better support from their church families. With our commitment to Christian values, theology, and actions, this book informs congregations on the issues and experiences that adoptees and their families face. It will offer guidance to churches on ways to include and embrace all those in the adoption circle.[4] Most importantly, it will facilitate the experience of belonging that adoptees and their families seek.

---

[4] The term adoption triad is used to identify the adoptee, first parents and adoptive parents as a group. Adoption constellation refers to these folks as well as extended family members in both birth and adoptive families.

To assist congregations and families this book introduces the concept of Adoption-attunement Quotient (AQ).[5] We coined this term to capture an important shift in the way we thought about and related to adoption and adoptees. It reflects both the concept of Multiple Intelligences[6] and "interpersonal attunement."[7] World-renowned neurobiologist Dr. Daniel Siegel describes interpersonal attunement as an effort "to examine how one person, a parent for example, focuses attention on the internal world of another, ... that enables two people to "feel felt" by each other. This state is crucial for people in relationships to feel vibrant and alive, to feel understood, and to feel at peace."[8] Siegel aligns with psychiatrist Dr. Steven Porges' belief that attunement builds a context of safety that frees people to "love without fear."[9] This attunes with Christian love—to love without fear, without restraint, without judgment.

Adoption necessitates an enhanced level of attunement that acknowledges the multi-faceted relationship challenges

---

[5] This book uses the abbreviation AQ* as shorthand for Adoption-attunement Quotient. It reflects the concept of multiple intelligences, for example, Intellectual (IQ,) Emotional (EQ.)

[6] Howard Gardner, Frames of Mind: The Theory of Multiple Intelligences, Basic Books; 3 edition, 2011

[7] Daniel J. Siegel, M.D., The Mindful Brain: Reflection and Attunement in the Cultivation of Well-Being (New York: WW Norton 2007)

[8] Siegel, op cit., page xii-xiv

[9] Siegel, op cit., page 130

caused by family fracture. These challenges complicate the effort to weave together the adoptive family. Attunement presupposes a commitment to harmony, to an awareness that values every element and allows each voice a chance to shine. Adoption-attunement threads through the entire book and is a foundational premise. AQ reflects a mindset that includes adoption-competence and also transcends it. A high AQ approach puts the adoptee at the hub. It lifts up adoptees, not the institution of adoption. AQ addresses the needs and actions of all involved. Like the notes in a soul-stirring symphony, every one matters.

Siegel asserts two significant points: first, the need "for each of us to be attuned to our own internal states in order to attune to others,"[10] and second, "attunement is not a luxury; it is a requirement of the individual to survive and thrive."[11] Within the context of adoptive family relationships this means parents must do their own internal work in order to fully meet the needs of their children. Within the context of faith families this means congregations and their staffs also must do internal work to meet the needs of their members. Good intentions must work hand in glove with accurate education. When one is out of tune, the whole is affected. Adoption-attunement strives for harmony within the shared relationship of all those touched by adoption.

The elements that compose Adoption-attunement are:

---

[10] Siegel, op cit., page 316

[11] Siegel, op cit., page 317

- Consider grief and loss issues
- Use sound adoption language
- Understand the attachment process
- Respect birth parents and first families
- Model, teach, and hold healthy boundaries
- Educate family, friends, teachers, and faith communities on adoption
- Remember a child's story belongs to him
- Recognize adoption as a family experience
- Encourage playfulness and good humor as a family value
- Integrate a child's birth heritage
- Honor a child's need to know and connect with birth family
- Nurture and value a child's innate talents, encourage her to be herself
- Recognize parents must work through their own grief and loss issues
- Follow ethical practices
- Operate with a child-centric focus

We firmly believe that as people and congregations learn and embrace Adoption-attunement, they will succeed in serving members of the adoption constellation.[12]

New ideas invite us to change. We acknowledge that change is hard. Yet Christians understand how a new order follows, fulfills, and replaces the old. (The pain of Good

---

[12] Adoption constellation defines a broader cluster of folks touched by adoption: the adoption triad plus their respective extended families.

Friday is replaced with the joy of the Resurrection!) Some of our assertions may startle you or be difficult to accept. Please keep an open mind as we lay out the reasons for our suggestions. We offer them in the spirit of love and we trust they will be received that way.

This awakening process takes time and commitment. This change in focus is necessary and worthwhile. Most importantly, it is the right thing to do.

We create the fertile soil for belonging by asking three fundamental questions.

In the past, what have we, The Church, done to make many adoptees and first families feel left out?

How are we including or excluding those in the adoption circle now?

What do we need to do in the future to make sure all feel as if they belong?

Reimagining Adoption: What Adoptees Seek from Families and Faith presents practical ways to lovingly support adoptees and their families—first *and* adoptive. This book is an act of radical advocacy: we assert that one of the best ways faith communities can support children and orphans is to reduce the number of adoptions in the first place. Adopt less not more. Address the factors that lead to adoption. Considering the painful realities that walk hand in hand with the benefits of family creation through adoption, we conclude that adoption should occur only when family preservation is impossible. Adoption should not be the first choice considered for a child in need of a stable loving family.

Reimagining Adoption: What Adoptees Seek from Families and Faith stands on the foundation of actual adoptee experiences and thoughts. Their stories are their gift to adoptive families. They have spoken clearly: Listen to us. Show us we belong.

> **"Love ... rejoices whenever the truth wins out..."**
> 1 Corinthians 13:6

CHAPTER 2

General Cultural Beliefs that Influence Adoption in America

Gayle's adult son described his evolving understanding of adoption like this. By age six he was quite familiar with the explanation of how his birth mother chose adoption for him. He began to wonder about the adoption stories of other children and expressed curiosity about his cousin's birth mother. Learning that his beloved aunt *was* his cousin's birth mother dumbfounded him. "You mean Auntie had to keep her?"

Until then he believed adoption was the norm. The revelation that some children remain with their birth parents—

unlike himself, his sibling, and most of his friends—upended his concept of family. His comment reveals that he viewed not being adopted as his cousin's loss. Eventually he learned the stark reality: most people are not adopted. He had gotten the short stick, not his cousin. That knowledge deepened throughout his life. The feelings of exclusion began in elementary school when his peers had taunted, "That birthmark on your face is because they couldn't clean you up after you were found abandoned on the sidewalk!" His young heart broke. (Where had his companions first heard such cruel thoughts expressed?)

His story shows how the message of being cherished and loved that he heard at home did not match the message he encountered elsewhere. The experience of Gayle's son illustrates the negative impact unhealthy cultural beliefs can have on a child.

This chapter unpacks cultural beliefs about adoption that may not be in our conscious awareness. They continue to be passed along without any evaluation for accuracy. Yet these beliefs influence all of our institutions—including The Church. We assert that these cultural beliefs are so engrained in our psyches that they have distorted the beliefs and practices of the Christian church and its members. When we examine this interconnectedness, we can understand and revise The Church's acts of welcome and hospitality toward adoptees and their families.

> *"People love to gloss over the relinquishment part of adoption and get right to the happy adoption story."* —Lynn G.

The Belief that America Knows Best and Is Best

Since the days of President Roosevelt our country has struggled with how much to influence other countries and people. At first, presidents wanted to bend every country to the American way and will. John Winthrop asserted that we should be a "city on a hill." Some interpreted that to mean that we should be a beacon for a sinful world. American author, journalist and academic Stephen Kinzer summarizes the superior attitude America often displays: "White people and Americans have a special gift for governing people around the world."[13]

This principle of American Exceptionalism continues to influence our country's basic mindset concerning adoption practices, especially as it pertains to white families who wish to adopt either domestically or internationally: that we have something better to offer children than their first family or country in which they currently live. The assumption sounds like this, *Adoptive parents can provide so much more—better food, superior education, increased opportunity; it's the brave choice, the wise choice, the loving choice.*

It is easy to look at children in difficult circumstances in developing countries—or even in pitiable situations in the United States—and presume that raising them out of poverty and a hard-scrabble life provides sufficient justification for fracturing families and placing children for adoption.

---

[13] Stephen Kinzer on 'America First' foreign policy: Then and now… https://www.mprnews.org/story/2018/04/05/america_first

But when the realities of adoption complexity also are factored into the decision-making, the choice becomes less clear cut. Poverty makes life difficult, but it does not make love impossible.

> *"It is spiritually abusive to use scripture to suggest a mother in need give her child a "better life" with someone more suitable in the church's mind...Help the mother and baby where they're at, don't help yourselves to her child."*
>
> — *Anonymous*

The Orphan Train movement of the Children's Home Society, with help of New York Foundling Hospital, was a striking example of using "we can give them a better life" to justify separating children from their first families. From 1854 to 1929, 100,000-250,000 children (some orphaned and some recruited from poor families) were taken from their families in New York City under the title, "Project of Salvation." Conferences that teach Christians how to start adoption ministries and use orphan care "to reach the world's unsaved people" still take place.[14]

In her book *The Child Catchers,* Kathryn Joyce reflects, "When speaking about the U.S. evangelical church, [missionaries] were duped by the peculiar strain of American evangelicalism that seems to think that the United States is God's chosen country and that seeks conversions by any and all means, including adoption...This has been taken to the extreme by theologians and pastors who encourage in-

---

[14] Joyce, The Child Catchers. 23, 43, 45

fertile couples to have the family of their dreams and expand the Kingdom at the same time by adopting a child from another culture and heritage and replacing that heritage and faith with their own...."[15]

Unfortunately, this stance of superiority can render the painful elements of adoption more tolerable for adoptive parents as well as communities as a whole. The thinking goes like this: If we have something better to give, then perhaps the trauma of separation, the destruction of a child's first family and culture is worth the cost.

While we want to share God's saving love with the world, our message needs to go hand-in-hand with a respect for other people's cultures, for their practices, and for their situations. We must engage with others with humility and recognize that we may not have all the answers. We may not know what is best or be the best solution. Our saving acts cannot be at the expense of first families and children. We must make every effort to ensure that the children we are helping truly have no family. This responsibility falls on the organizations facilitating adoptions, as well as on families who wish to adopt.

> *"I would really like to say "stop using adoption as a cause to win souls." —Lynn G.*

Belief: We Deserve the Family of Our Dreams

---

[15] Joyce, Kathryn. Child Catchers. Public Affairs. New York. 2013.

Most of us absorbed cultural presuppositions about family during our childhoods. Dreams of our adult selves included images of us as parents.

Sally felt called to be a parent. She dreamed of what a family Christmas photo would look like: she and her husband with children sitting on their laps and their arms lovingly wrapped around them—all wearing color-coordinated outfits. She pictured owning a mini-van with the stick-family decal on the back window, complete with a dog and a cat. They would be family. A beautiful single unit that offered the best chance for their children to be happy and flourish.

Life does not always turn out the way we fantasized. Reality often varies significantly from the dream. Families fall apart. Pregnancies miscarry or never happen in the first place. Still, we hold on to the dream. This is when thoughts typically turn to adoption.

Before they married, Gayle and George knew that she could not bear children. On the other hand, Sally and Dan always had intended to adopt. Infertility caused them to choose adoption as the sole way of creating their family. For both families the dream to become parents took on consuming urgency. Those who knew and loved them ached for them and joined their prayers. When their children arrived, family, friends, and colleagues celebrated with them. They believed, as did Sally and Gayle, that adoption blessed their children and themselves.

Most adoptive parents feel this drive to have a family.

•27 REIMAGINING ADOPTION: WHAT ADOPTEES SEEK FROM FAMILIES AND FAITH•

> *"Adoption is traumatic and I wish more people would realize this."* –Lisa F.

Adoptees do not share this same fantasy. They wonder why they had to lose their birth family, heritage, and place along the family time line. A child is not a blank slate so they feel great anguish over this loss of first family. When he joins his new family, he carries with him memories, emotions, a psyche, and a soul. His DNA retains a blueprint which reflects a biological truth through which his ancestral lineage will continue to flow. Adoption is a sacred commitment of the heart and a legal contract. But it cannot alter DNA. This means an adopted child cannot become the embodiment of their adopted parents' imagined biological child. It is cruel to impose this impossible expectation. Nurture certainly enhances or diminishes the inclinations of nature, but it cannot erase them.

When we overemphasize the idea that we can provide a child with the best environment—a traditional family—we easily can slide into presupposing that an adoptive family is the best outcome for a child. We may then minimize the loss of the child's first family and dismiss the serious consequences and agony of early maternal/child separation that occur in adoption. This misplaced focus on the benefits of an adoptive family may tempt us not to work hard enough to avert these losses. We may avoid asking questions that could reveal—when all factors are considered—that an adoptive home may not be the optimum environment for a child.

Chapter 2:
General Cultural Beliefs that Influence Adoption in America

We may believe that adoption is right for our child. Unfortunately, our adherence to the "rightness" of our stance can bias our thoughts. Bias can lead us to justify unsavory methods to produce our desired results. It can tempt us into dismissing shady means as a "necessary cost" of accomplishing our goal.[16]

People who are desperate to have children may be willing to pay huge sums of money to create their family. This practice has given rise to a thriving industry with children as the commodity and prospective parents as the consumer. The adoption industry helps prospective parents market themselves to expectant mothers. Some hopeful parents hold events to raise money to fund an adoption. Such efforts have proliferated on the internet. One of those sites, AdoptTogether.org reports that it has raised over $12.6 million dollars in five years.[17] In fact, The Daily Dot reports that "crowdsourcing is the future of adoption."[18]

Many of us may have viewed a popular adoption-awareness television program that showcased children desperate for homes and then featured the families who adopted these children. Two messages come across clearly. First: now all is well, and second: viewers should open their hearts to other children who are "out there waiting." The

---

[16] The Child Finders, Rescue, Trafficking and the New Gospel of Adoption by Kathryn Joyce, Public Affairs, New York, page 35

[17] Aaron Sankin, "Crowdsourcing is the Future of Adopting." https://www.dailydot.com/irl/open-adoption-internet-crowdsourcing/ Jan 7, 2014

[18] https://adopttogether.org/about/

focus is on helplessness and rescue. These programs can play on the heartstrings of childless families or those who want to rescue. While many children truly need homes, the portrayal lacks an acknowledgment of first families and can shed—through silence—a negative light on first parents.

Many of the adoptees who responded to our survey expressed great pain regarding The Church's role in facilitating adoptions especially during the Baby Scoop Era.[19] Most felt let down by the lack of effort expended to keep first families intact. They see prospective adoptive parents having fundraisers for adoption expenses that can run from n$30,000.00 to $40,000.00 or even higher.[20] They wish a fraction of that effort, money, and support might have been spent to keep original families intact.

An adoptee activist reacts with this perspective.

Fundraising:

"When people who are too poor to adopt

Raise money to adopt a child of a woman too poor to parent."
—Stephanie M.

---

[19] https://en.wikipedia.org/wiki/Baby_Scoop_Era The Baby Scoop Era occurred between 1945-1973. During these years, women were coerced by social, religious, and family mores to surrender their babies conceived out of wedlock and place them for adoption.

[20] Child Welfare Information Gateway. (2016). Planning for adoption: Knowing the costs and resources. Washington, DC: U.S. Department of Health and Human Services, Children's Bureau.

Others felt utterly betrayed by The Church's definite preference for adoption and blindness to the psychological, emotional, and spiritual price of adoption, and by The Church's—and their surrogates—choosing to view adoption through a filter that saw only the benefits. One respondent wrote:

> *"Lutheran Child and Family Services sold me in 1967 for $250.00 to a "nice Christian couple...My 'faith community' sold me for profit." —Jeannie V.*

We must be as dedicated to keeping vulnerable families together as we are eager to help prospective adoptive parents find children. Otherwise, careful investigation to ensure this child truly is without a first family can fall by the wayside. As the number of children available for adoption continues to decrease, the chances for further exploitation may increase. We must stop the objectification of children. We must not reduce children to problems in need of a solution or projects in need of rescue. Adoption is not always the best solution. Sometimes it is not even a good solution.

Further, we must never lose sight of the trauma that underpins all adoption: the separation of the child from his/her mother. Nancy Verrier wrote extensively on this in her seminal book, *The Primal Wound*. This wound occurs even in kinship (intra-family) adoption because the relationship fracture still occurs.

> *"Any time a child is severed from his family it is a tragedy that is life-long and affects not just the child but the entire family for generations." —Sandy B.*

Belief: Adoption Is All Good, Yet Inferior

Traditionally, the culture at large and most faith communities have viewed adoption through a lens of monolithic positivity. They painted it as a win/win/win that benefits all parties involved. Sealed records locked birth and adoptive families behind opposite sides of a permanent barrier. The cultural belief asserted that this was in the best interest of all, that a clean cut made it easier. (It turns out that it did not make it easier, not for the children, not for the first parents, and to some extent, not for the adoptive families either.)[21]

Because the pain of family fracture went unseen, unspoken, and unacknowledged it was logical for faith communities and society to empathize and over-identify with the plight of the childless couple yearning for a family or the "selfless" couple seeking to provide a family to a child in need of one. Many people offered comfort and support for the pain (shame?) of infertility. Adoptive parents routinely received effusive praise for adopting. Since loving a child is not an extraordinary thing to do, one must read between the lines to look for the source of this "admirable" aspect.

People view adoption as heroic because they see it as something they could not or would not choose. Their reluctance indicates an unspoken judgment that something is

---

[21] Open access is supported by Groups like North American Council on Adoptable Children, The Donaldson Institute, American Association for Adoption Attorneys, American Adoption Congress, etc.

inherently inferior about adopted children and that adoptive families are not quite as attached, as real, or as good as families built through good, old-fashioned biology.

This assessment often comes packaged in demeaning, backhanded compliments: *You are so brave. Are you afraid they'll be like their parents? I could never love a child that was not mine. Do you still hope to have a child of your own?*

Adopted children and even adult adoptees receive a barrage of offensive conversations, unsolicited advice, and rude commentary. One of the most frequently proffered admonitions: they should feel lucky that they were adopted.

We must never forget that to receive the "blessing" of an adopted family, the adoptee had to lose his/her first family. That loss is anything but lucky. Even when caused by abuse and neglect, any time a child is separated from his family of origin, it is a tragedy. We cannot continue to use sanitizing language to obscure the very real personal cost of adoption.

Belief: Birth Mothers and Birth Families Should and Can Forget

Each of these souls—child, first parents, and adoptive parents but especially first mothers—was expected to move forward from the moment of adoption and never look back. Prevailing sentiment saw adoption as a positive solution for both the child and the adoptive parents albeit a difficult one for the birth mother. Especially in the Baby Scoop Era (1945-1970s) a pregnant girl was expected to tough it out, swallow the pain, and release her child to adoption. Faith communities and often families, as well, saw the expectant mother's situation as evidence of poor judgment, a shameful fact that needed to be hidden, and a moral failure that merited the loss of her child.

Hiding the child's birth also prevented the world from learning the family had a "fallen woman" in their ranks. Their daughter's "betrayal" of the family's reputation remained a secret never. To ensure that the family shame remained hidden, no one mentioned the baby again. The mother received no comfort in her grief. No one validated or acknowledged her tremendous loss. No one shared her mourning of her lost child. She was expected to be happy and relieved. All efforts concentrated on sustaining the lie, on covering up her sin, and on pretending the child never existed. No one rallied around the mother to help her keep her baby. The primary focus was on hiding the birth—the evidence of her sin. Loss of her child was deemed an appropriate penance.

Some degree of taint attached to the children and thus some states—but not all—created amended birth certificates to hide the children's bastardy. Too young to have a say, the babies were voiceless pawns whose lives were changed immeasurably by adoption. They were lopped off one family tree and grafted to another.

Women who got cold feet faced pressure to complete the adoption. In some cases clergy counseled them that keeping their babies would mean their children could "never be baptized in the church."[22] Other women reported that when they attempted to keep their babies, the maternity home presented them with enormous bills to cover hospital fees for themselves and their newborns and repay foster parents.[23] Since lack of adequate resources, especially financial resources, had caused them to consider adoption in the first place, this kind of monetary pressure left them no choice. When they surrendered their babies to be adopted the bills disappeared.

Sadly, such coercive practices were common during this time period. Women were counseled to be "unselfish," to do the "right" thing—to choose adoption. Relinquishment, they were told, was the most selfless and brave demonstration of their love for their children. Forget these children. Future babies will replace them. Birth mothers eventually learned that forgetting their children would be the real sin; moreover, it was impossible. Like Peter hearing the cock's crow after he denied Jesus, they knew the soul-deep weight of guilt and shame that haunted them when they erased their children from their "public" life histories. The impenetrable wall that separated birth families and adoptees affected them all.

---

[22] Fessler, Ann. The Girls Who Went Away: The Hidden History of Women Who Surrendered Children for Adoption in the Decades before Roe v. Wade. Penguin Books; Reprint edition (June 26, 2007), 17

[23] Fessler, 91

REIMAGINING ADOPTION: WHAT ADOPTEES SEEK FROM FAMILIES AND FAITH

Secrecy and shame, sealed records, and severed relationships defined American adoption practices. Isolation deepened an adoptee's pain of abandonment, yet it did not erase his/her primal connection to his/her first families. Reduced to ghost status, birth parents and birth families still occupied adoptees' thoughts, dreams, and longings even if they did not feel free to voice them aloud.[24]

First families remained influential and vital to adoptees on a psychic and emotional level whether or not they retained any contact or were allowed to express those thoughts and yearnings.

Birth mothers, adult adoptees, and their families came to understand the "cost" of adoption to both child and mother: the promised closure, peace of mind, and "forgetting" never happened, so they spoke out in increasing numbers. Social mores softened and adoption professionals and facilitators listened to these impassioned stories. Attitudes and policies began to change. Adoption statistics reveal a profound shift: "In 1970, approximately 80% of the infants born to single mothers were ... [taken for adoption purposes], whereas by 1983 that figure had dropped to only 4%."][25] Notice that once women felt "allowed" to keep and

---

[24] Lifton, Betty Jean. Quoted in Clinical and Practice Issues in Adoption--Revised and Updated: Bridging the Gap between Adoptees Placed as Infants and as Older Children, Victor Groza, editor, Karen F. Rosenberg Praeger; Revised, Updated edition. 2001.

[25] Brodzinsky, A. (1994). "Surrendering an Infant for Adoption: The Birthmother Experience". In The Psychology of Adoption, D. Brozinsky and M. Schechter (Eds.). New York: Oxford University Press. (p. 297)

parent their children, they did so in great numbers. Families stayed intact which is surely a positive result.

When we provide women with adequate support and resources, most opt to keep their children. These resources assist in family preservation *and significantly reduce the pressure for women to seek abortion.* This is a very desirable result. Keeping families intact also improves the mental health and quality of life for first mothers.[26]

Many birth mothers also face significant emotional upheaval after placing a child for adoption. They struggle with depression, shame, unresolved grief, and worry about their placed children.[27] So much for win/win/win. Adoption blends gains with losses. They do not cancel each other out; they coexist. First mothers need and deserve more compassion and less judgment from society, their own families, and The Church. They are suffering and have been grossly underserved and unsupported. We must channel Christian love and encouragement and leave the judgment to God.

> *"What kind of God wants mothers to suffer?"* —Anonymous

Belief: Adoption Takes Away the Pain of Infertility

---

[26] "Impact of Adoption on Birth Parents," https://www.childwelfare.gov/pubPDFs/f_impact.pdf

[27] American Journal of Orthopsychiatry © 2014 American Orthopsychiatric Association, 2014, Vol. 84, No. 4, 409–419 http://dx.doi.org/10.1037/ort0000013

REIMAGINING ADOPTION: WHAT ADOPTEES SEEK FROM FAMILIES AND FAITH

Adoptees and first parents are not the only ones confronting grief and loss. Infertility—the most common reason driving people to opt for adoption—also carries a legacy of loss and emotional pain. Although adoptive parents are no longer childless, they are still infertile. This reality can have repercussions in family relationships. Unless handled they can have significant, unconscious impact on the family dynamics.

In addition to infertility, people adopt for other reasons, for example, a call to serve, a declaration of faith, a desire to be a single parent, etc. Whether or not infertility drove their decisions, all adoptive parents lack a biological link to their adopted child. The lack of a genetic link is a loss whether parents consciously grieve this reality or not.

Some adoptees reported feeling that their adoptive parents adopted as an obligation of faith and not out of desire to parent the adoptee. Adoption was a cross they had to bear, and a transaction done out of Christian duty not out of love. We can easily see how this transactional foundation shapes the relationship and creates an impediment to attachment. Every child deserves to feel his/her arrival in the family was an event passionately desired and fervently celebrated. This stands in stark contrast to feeling one is a burden his parents felt obligated to shoulder.

> *"People should only adopt if they actually want to parent, not because they think it is their duty."—Anonymous*

Adoptive parents anticipate that they will shape their (adopted) children. Many give little thought to how children will also reflect influences of their first family's heritage. In fact, children may differ significantly from the adoptive family in temperament, aptitude, stature, and stamina. Parents must ensure that they nurture the child they have and not attempt to confine and reshape him into the historical patterns of the adoptive family.

Equally important, the adoptive family and faith community must affirm the child's abiding need for knowledge and connection to his biological roots. They must value and honor the ways children are like the adoptive family as well as the ways in which they differ. Nurture collaborates with nature; it is additive, not subtractive.

> *"My life is an emotional challenge of balancing two very different families and two very different sides of myself."*
> —Rebekah H.

Cultural Practices That Can Exclude Adoptees and Their Families

Saying or Believing Adoptees Are Broken

Many people mistakenly believe that adoptees are bad seeds, broken, and/or damaged. The truth about adoption is both simpler and more complex. They are burdened, not broken. Life dealt them a tough hand and they struggle to cope within the parameters of trauma. They are not damaged but they do face additional developmental tasks. They must figure out how to construct a single, cohesive identity from their dual heritages.

39 REIMAGINING ADOPTION: WHAT ADOPTEES SEEK FROM FAMILIES AND FAITH

Adoption places profound, life-long challenges on adoptees and first families. It exacts tolls physically, emotionally, and spiritually. Responses to adoption-generated challenges vary widely and are unique to each individual and to the complexity of their personal situation. Adoptees can never become "unadopted." They must cope with the fallout for their entire lives. The initial loss cannot be erased whether the adoption is open or closed.[28] Even after reunion—whether successful or not for adoptees or first parents—the years lost can never be recaptured. Adoptees and first parents demonstrate a range of resiliency. Some develop coping strategies that push people away. Some hold themselves to impossible standards of perfection.

Open Adoption first became normalized in the 1980's. Currently most adoptions include some degree of openness. Faith communities can update their perception of adoption as an entirely closed experience and embrace this shift as a reflection of expanded belonging which God's desire for healing and wholeness would encourage.

Openness in adoption does not necessarily equate with full physical contact; it is a spectrum of connection, contact, and shared interactions. Often it evolves over time. It always should be based on respect, truthfulness, and the drive to serve the child's best interest. All relationships are

---

[28] A 2008 survey of 100 domestic private agencies with infant adoption programs found that over the past 2 years only 5 percent of infant adoptions were closed, 55 percent were open, and 40 percent were mediated (Siegel & Smith, 2012). The percentage of adoptions in which contact is maintained varies over time. Child Welfare Information Gateway. Available online at https://www.childwelfare.gov/pubs/f_openadoptbulletin.cfm, Child

complicated. Open adoptions, by their very nature and the number of people involved, are innately thorny. Each party has his/her personal loss, needs, desires, and personalities. It takes heroic dedication and the highest degree of personal integrity to make it work. The logistics are not easy; however, in most cases open adoption offers the healthiest approach.

With all the challenges they face it is no wonder adoptees and their families yearn to be able to rely on their faith communities for non-judgmental, well-informed support.

Using Adoption as a Label

Adoptees report that people routinely tag them as being adopted. Labeling a person as an adoptee violates his fundamental right to privacy because it reveals his personal information without his permission. Adoptees should decide when and with whom they wish to share their adoptive status. This gratuitous label establishes a hurtful sense of "otherness." Usually when people add adoption as a qualifier—adopted child, adopted parent—they intend to draw a distinction. In almost every case, the distinction is unnecessary. So, what compels them to highlight the fact?

Tagging serves to identify adoption as the root cause for something—almost always something negative. Friends, neighbors, and even the extended family all engage in this speech pattern. *Johnnie is in trouble. Again. He's adopted, you know.* Or, with raised eyebrows they whisper, *Jane is such a handful. She's adopted. Her parents are saints.*

The implied criticism is not lost on adoptees. They "get the message" that society suspects they are inferior, that adopting them is risky, that their parents are brave to take them in, that they were "second choice." The words land on a very raw emotional hotspot: adoptees' own inner fear that they are in fact inferior, rejection-worthy, and that this innate inferiority caused their birth families to reject them in the first place.

> *"Once I saw an announcement in church that someone's 'adopted child' was being baptized. That made me really angry on behalf of the child."* —Megan D.

Media portrayals of adoption influence people's opinion of adoptees. (It also influences adoptees' opinion of themselves.) When characters joke that a sibling is so weird he must be adopted, the implied negative judgment about adoption comes across clearly. Screenplays that express parental disappointment in their child with lines like, "He must be adopted; at least I hope so," reinforce the stereotype of adoption as inferior. Likewise, cheap-shot jokes that make adoption the punchline are equally destructive and unkind. "If only he were adopted, you could give him back." If you were an adoptee, how would these words make you feel?

Conflating Adoption and Abortion

Many people think about adoption as the abortion alternative. They often suggest to adoptees that they were fortunate to be adopted instead of aborted. Adoptees know their birth parents may have considered abortion. But it is important to note that many first mothers report that they *never* considered abortion. For them the choice was never between adoption and abortion; it was between parenting and adoption.

> "I would encourage faith communities to cease looking at us as though we are products of sin who are lucky to be alive, and should be grateful we were not terminated."
>
> —Jeff H.

It is also possible our own biological parents may have considered abortion when they became pregnant with us. What? Sounds crazy but only our [birth] parents know the answer.

Now imagine a time when you were facing personal family problems and having people say to you, "At least your parents decided not to abort you." The absurdity of their comments would confound and probably offend you. Certainly, you would not find comfort or support in such words. Yet people routinely say such things to adoptees and they expect appreciation for their offensive sentiments and unsolicited advice.

> "Do not advocate "adoption over abortion" as if there are only two choices; the most obvious is to care for the birth mother and make sure she keeps her child but rarely does this come into play." —Nicole N.

The National Council for Adoption calculates the adoption rate as 1.7% and the abortion rate as 27.4%. Reducing unplanned pregnancy offers a more effective way to reduce abortion rates.[29]

In summary, congregations and their faithful members live within the society that has created these foundational cultural beliefs, practices, and barriers. More than we may realize, our understanding and interpretation of Scripture have been influenced by our society's beliefs about adoption.

Inadequate understanding of the cultural factors involved, of the gravity and generations-long effects of adoption can magnify the perceived benefits and minimize—even overlook or trivialize—the costs to adoptees and first families. Overemphasizing the needs of the prospective adoptive parents at the expense of the rights and needs of the expectant parents can skew the way faith communities counsel and affect everything from how we approach adoptees to the responses and resources we offer women experiencing an unplanned or crisis pregnancy.

Faith communities operate many ministries to address the needs of members and to live out the mission of their beliefs. We know that faith families want to serve their constituencies well. Their honorable motives and good intentions must be grounded in a deep understanding of the needs of those seeking help. People must be able to rely on the church for appropriate, skilled and ethical guidance—without a pre-determined bias in favor of adoption. When it

---

[29] http://www.adoptioncouncil.org/publications/2017/02/adoption-by-the-numbers

comes to adoption, all support must be Adoption-attuned. Otherwise, it can inflict more harm than good.

> *"The church needs to be a place of understanding—a sanctuary community—a place where adoptees can be free to share their story without fear of being labeled "ungrateful. A place that helps them put the pieces of the puzzle together."* —Carla B.

Times have changed. In order for The Church to create a genuine space for belonging, we must bear in mind the influence of our American culture while we look at foundational scriptural interpretations and beliefs. Then we must take the time to rethink them based on solid theological review. From there we can update our concepts, beliefs, and practices surrounding adoption.

Adoptees want to be able to turn to their churches, to feel supported, and to feel as if they belong. The following chapters will help us do this.

Questions to Consider

1. How do cultural beliefs affect the attitudes and practices regarding adoption?
2. In what ways do you see our cultural beliefs influencing your own understanding of family and adoption?
3. How has your understanding of adoption shifted?
4. How do grief and loss shape the lives of adoptive and first families?

Steps to Take:

1. Reexamine your beliefs about adoption, the forces which drive it, the benefits anticipated, and losses which underpin it.

2. Do not over-glorify adoption or minimize the losses experienced by adoptees, first parents, and adoptive parents.

3. Be sensitive when discussing adoption.

CHAPTER 3

Cultural Belief: That Adoptees Do Not Need To Know about Their Birth Families

> *"We have two families...Lean in to adoptee rights. Lean in to giving adoptees more love from every family member rather than cutting us (and our descendants) off from our families and our heritage."* –T.V.

This cultural belief deserves its own chapter because the fallout from this belief touches the very core of an adoptee's sense of self-worth and right to exist.

As women raised in their biological families, Sally and Gayle take some everyday events for granted. When they visit their folks, all their senses weave a message: they are home. They feel it in their mothers' familiar smell and tender embrace. They hear it in their dads' laughter and thought patterns. They notice their parents in themselves.

Even if families were difficult, chaotic, or painful, those raised by their biological families at least know their first families. They can take what they want and make it their own, reject the parts they do not want, and attempt to heal from the pains.

Step into an adoptee's shoes. Imagine not having this template, this enfolding, reassuring knowledge and sense of belonging. Imagine having little or no information about one's birth parents. Imagine having only "what ifs", but no factual answers. Imagine knowing one's first family but not living with them. This exercise allows us to open our hearts and minds to challenge the belief that adoptees do not need their first families.

The strength of a building depends on the stability of its base. Human beings need a firm foundation, too. They have an innate desire to know where they fit in the flow of their family story. Hence, websites like Ancestry.com proliferate to fill this thirst for knowledge and for connection to one's roots. Abraham Maslow considered Love and Belonging as the third most important element in man's Hierarchy of Needs.[30] Knowledge of one's genealogical history is an essential ingredient to create that sense of belonging. (We

---

[30] https://www.simplypsychology.org/maslow.html, Maslow determined five essential needs: physiological, safety, love and belonging, esteem and self-actualization.

would assert that adoptees have a sixth need—the need for adoption-attunement—and that it must be present for them to feel safe.) Genealogical information supports and stabilizes us. It provides an anchor that roots us in the flow of time and is a vital element in the scaffold on which we build our identity.

This thirst for knowing where one fits in the unfolding of the generations has deep roots in Christian narrative. The Bible includes a strong emphasis on genealogy. For example, Genesis 5[31] lists the generations of Adam. It goes to great lengths to demonstrate Jesus' lineage through the house of David.

> *"I've spent most of my life trying to straddle both sides of the fence of being the perfect, grateful daughter and the heartbroken girl who felt unloved, unwanted, and unworthy." —Anonymous*

The universal desire to establish one's genealogical history is powerful which accounts for the popularity of two highly successful television series.[32] Each episode features guests who are visibly moved when they rediscover lost family history and lineages. Like the rest of us, adoptees crave this knowledge and security. They neither lose nor abrogate this desire just because they were adopted. In fact, they need it even more because their biological

---

[31] King James Version

[32] "Who Do You Think You Are" ran for eleven seasons on TLC. "Find Your Roots" is currently in its fifth season on PBS.

roots have been severed and because they have more elements to assemble into a healthy and cohesive whole. Most importantly, they want the truth. Their truth.

About ten years ago Sally's sister, who was adopted in the late 1960's, was experiencing medical issues that caused her to consider asking for information about her first family of which she knew nothing. This reignited her curiosity. Her desire for knowledge of her first family's health history fueled Sally's sister's desire to know more about herself by knowing more about them. Her inquiry began with a phone call to the social service agency that had placed her with Sally's parents more than 30 years ago.

Sally cannot even imagine what was going through her sister's mind as she finally decided to make that call. Sally's sister began by asking, "I am wondering how I go about getting my adoption records."

The woman responded in a matter-of-fact tone. Sally's sister was so stunned by what she heard next; she cannot remember the exact comment. She does recall, however, that the total amount of $1,000 was necessary just to start the process of record-finding and searching for both of her first parents. For her sister the response was enough for her to stop her search.

From an observer's point of view and as one who loves her sister, Sally thought, *How has it happened that people have to ask permission to know about themselves and pay money—significant amounts of it—to find out where they come from and who they are?*

> *"Faith teaches us to be honest. This should carry over to the way we approach adoptees. It's our right to know who we are."* –Lynn. M

Adoptees have been told that searching is impolite, unappreciative, and out of bounds. Both family and faith communities have suggested—expected—them not to need the connection to their family history. Adoptees report that this expectation ignores their needs and contributes to their feeling rootless, unmoored, and vulnerable.

Some adoptees describe the cultural expectations surrounding adoption as boxing them into a place where they are not allowed to describe the full range of their adoption-related thoughts, emotions, experiences, and desires because it does not align with the rosy cultural picture that prevails. They feel pressured to remain silent and to keep their trauma hidden. They express particular frustration and pain when it is their faith communities who exact this requirement of silence to reinforce this rosy picture.

> *"My faith community substituted its version of the truth for my own needs to search and know my origins."* —T. V.

Adoptees describe their experience as a type of "gaslighting." (This term is taken from psychology. It refers to "manipulation that seeks to sow seeds of doubt in a targeted individual or in members of a targeted group, hoping to make them question their own memory, perception, and sanity. Using persistent denial, misdirection, contradiction, and lying, it attempts to destabilize the target and delegitimize the target's belief.")[33] While neither the dominant culture nor faith communities consciously use gaslighting, the practice and attitudes about adoption have historically operated in a way that strongly prefers the idealized tale to the complex truth.

Many adoptees say in order to retain their acceptance within their adoptive and faith families, they have felt compelled to suppress and/or deny the hard stuff of adoption. Fulfilling this requirement has proven physically and psychologically damaging. In many cases, it drives a wedge between adoptees and their families, as well as between adoptees and their faith. Although unintended, this division occurs in significant numbers. The psychic stress is undeniable: statistics reveal that adoptees commit suicide at four times the rate of non-adopted persons.[34] They also demonstrate an elevated risk of substance abuse. Adoption is not the sole cause of these behaviors. In fact, the lack of validation of their experiences, the pressure to suppress their adoption-related losses and other life challenges also may contribute.

Secrets do not foster truth. By their very existence they imply that something must be hidden, something shameful, something too ugly to be known, spoken in whispers if discussed at all. Secrets deepen the shame adoptees often feel already. World-renowned trauma expert Dr. Peter

---

[33] https://en.wikipedia.org/wiki/Gaslighting

[34] http://pediatrics.aappublications.org/content/early/2013/09/04/peds.2012-3251

Levine says, "Shame is like a cancer ... Shame doesn't exist in isolation... It exists first in relationship betrayal." From a child's innocent eyes and youthful perspective, what could be more shameful than his birth mother's rejection? Most young adoptees experience these worries. They hide them even from their adoptive parents because they are afraid they might jeopardize their place in their adoptive family. When they need the love, comfort, and support of their parents the most, fear leaves them afraid to ask for it. Adult adoptees say that this emotional tug of war continues to dog them into adulthood.

Adoptees struggle under the weight of secrecy and shame. It exacerbates their feelings of rootlessness, of feeling othered, rejected, and unwanted. Sealed records leave them wobbly and off kilter, like a chair with half of its legs missing.

"God does not seal records." —*Elle C.*

Advocate for Truth

While people readily understand why non-adopted people pursue family genealogy, adoptees have been expected to relinquish this urge to know their truth. Adoption does not, cannot change human nature.

As Christians, the Ten Commandments serve as our Rule Book for Life. The Ninth Commandment obligates us to truthfulness. Because of our deep-rooted commitment to truth, Christians will want to support adult adoptees' rights

CULTURAL BELIEF: THAT ADOPTEES DO NOT NEED TO KNOW ABOUT THEIR BIRTH FAMILIES

to access their original birth certificates. Truth provides freedom to adoptees. Instead of worrying about every possibility—terrible, magical, or something in between, they only need to handle what is actually true. Whether harsh or easy, it is their story, their truth, their burden to carry.

Ronald J. Nydam, Assistant Professor of Pastoral Care at Calvin Seminary writes, "Knowing their stories no matter how painful the stories may be is liberating in a way that sets adoptees free to truly be themselves. But the knowing does not come without the hurting."[35] Thus, the need to know the facts does not render difficult information painless. Adoptees need support as they labor to incorporate the elements of their personal story. When faith communities step in to provide support, it must be with a highly attuned sensitivity that reflects a High AQ.

> *"I was always conflicted and skeptical that religion had my best interests at heart when it sought to separate me from my truth. Rather than support me in my search for it."*
> —T. V.

Sealed records block adoptees from their rightful information and are an anachronism in the era of the internet and social media. Faith communities can embrace movements like Adoptee Rights Coalition which advocates for the passage of legislation permitting the adult adoptee access to records. (Be sure to follow IRS parameters.) Nydam adds, "The cry of the adoptee in our society is not simply a

---

[35] Nydam, Ronald J., Adoptees Come of Age: Living within Two Families. Westminster John Knox Press, Louisville, 1999, page 45

complaint about emotional and spiritual suffering, it is also a demand for fairness in the classroom."[36]

Psychologists, social workers, and most importantly adoptees are united in their demand for access to their own unredacted records instead of amended birth certificates. Although they are legal documents, amended birth certificates actually document a lie as the truth. They attest that the adoptive parents gave birth to the adoptee—even in cases where children were adopted from foster care and have intact memories of their biological parents. This is both absurd and false. It also totally contravenes the commandment not to bear false witness.

Gayle and her husband received the amended birth certificate for their son—their first child—they were shocked to discover they were not listed as adoptive parents. The certificate intentionally conveyed the idea they'd given birth to him. They found this quite ironic for three reasons. One, they weren't present at his birth. Two, neither of them had served in the military; yet their son had been born at the naval base. Three, Gayle had a complete hysterectomy at age fifteen because of ovarian cancer. Now that is what one could certainly call a miraculous birth! Certified. Official. False. They would have been quite satisfied with a Certificate of Adoption that listed us as the adoptive mother and adoptive father. This would have been truthful and could still have validated his date and place of birth. Certainly, by the time an adoptee has reached adulthood, no

---

[36] Ibid., page 6

CULTURAL BELIEF: THAT ADOPTEES DO NOT NEED TO KNOW ABOUT THEIR BIRTH FAMILIES

further reason exists for hiding the facts of his parentage from him.

"Closed" adoptions—those in which the first and adoptive parents remain anonymous to one another—dwindled to approximately 5% of adoptions arranged in 2008.[37] Most people are surprised to learn that sealed records are not a long-established norm. According to the Adoption History Project conducted by the University of Oregon, "Until 1945, however, most members of adoptive families in the United States had perfectly legal access to birth certificates and adoption-related court documents and most agencies acted as passive registries through which separated relatives might locate one another. Disclosure—not secrecy—has been the historical norm in adoption."[38]

Adult adoptees want and deserve access to their original birth certificates and the true information which it contains. As adults they believe they have the right, maturity, and ability to handle their truth. As adults they want to make their own determination on this decision. Sealed records mean they are never considered old enough to know what is hidden, purportedly in their best interest. Adult adoptees insist that they need not be sheltered from the facts of these

---

[37] Carp, E. Wayne (1992) "The Sealed Adoption Records Controversy in Historical Perspective: The Case of the Children's Home Society of Washington, 1895-1988," The Journal of Sociology & Social Welfare: Vol. 19: Iss. 2, Article 5. Available at: http://scholarworks.wmich.edu/jssw/vol19/iss2/5

[38] http://darkwing.uoregon.edu/~adoption/topics/confidentiality.htm
The Adoption History Project, please contact Ellen Herman, Department of History, University of Oregon, Eugene, Oregon 97403-1288

relationships. They demand release from their status as "permanent children" who—regardless of their age—are barred from accessing their own data.

> *"I am 69 years-old but treated as a child, baby by the Catholic Family Services."* —John C.

Many adoptees wrestle with a significant fear: the possibility that they might unwittingly date or marry a sibling or close biological relative. In closed adoptions this is a possibility that has occurred with heartbreaking results.

When adoption becomes necessary, everyone involved must follow the highest ethical standards. This includes not only those with whom the church has direct control but also anyone peripherally involved. We cannot use unethical practices to accomplish our good intentions. We can and must use our collective power to insist on ethics in action. It is the just and moral thing to do.

Faith communities can educate staff and parishioners on this issue and allow their consciences to guide them to action. Imagine yourself as an adoptee. Wouldn't you want to know the truth? Access to Original Birth Certificates (OBCs) is both reasonable and just; it is mentally, spiritually, and physically healthier for adoptees. Just as parents love all their children, adoptees want, need, and deserve to nurture all of their familial relationships. When they cannot obtain the information through open records, what recourse do they have? Just as Solomon had the wisdom to know the true mother would not want to split the baby in two, we

CULTURAL BELIEF: THAT ADOPTEES DO NOT NEED TO KNOW ABOUT THEIR BIRTH FAMILIES

cannot expect adoptees to split themselves in two and limit their access to only one half.

Records can be unsealed but the process is complicated and requires adoptees to "prove" their need to access the information. Some can hire attorneys to advocate on their behalf in a case-by-case approach. This is costly and, therefore, leaves many—like Sally's sister—unable to use this option. Success is not guaranteed; in fact, it is the exception, not the norm.

Adoptees and first parents turn to social networks like Facebook where they post a very public plea for information. So much for keeping things private. Their need to know forms a powerful driving force and for most adoptees it is a need they feel utterly compelled to fill. Open records offer a more humane, respectful, and private way to access their stories without having to resort to splashing their personal information all over the internet.

> *"I [my faith community] sought to separate me from my truth, rather than support me in my search for it... Lean in to giving adoptees more love from every family member rather than cutting us (and our descendants) off from our families and heritage."* —T. V.

This re-envisioned stance of openness and advocacy for truth models a pathway forward for others to follow.

Questions to Consider

1. How has this chapter opened your mind to new ways of supporting adoptees?

2. What are you willing to do to help adoptees gain access to their original birth certificates?

3. What can you do to create a sense of safety and acceptance for adoptees and their families within your faith community?

Steps to Take

1. Advocate for truth.
2. Validate the full spectrum of adoption experience.
3. Ensure ethical practices.

Chapter 4

Scriptural Interpretation Supported the Fracture of Families

> "But now thus says the LORD, he who created you, O Jacob, he who formed you, O Israel: Fear not, for I have redeemed you; I have called you by name, you are mine."
> —Isaiah 43:1 [39]

In the previous chapters, we explored several cultural beliefs and practices that have influenced how we, as The

---

[39] https://www.biblegateway.com/verse/en/Isaiah%2043:1

Church, have understood Scripture and church practices in light of adoption. It is complicated, certainly. Yet an examination is worth it for adoptees and their families—as well as for the integrity of The Church and its faithfulness to God's Word.

The Funeral That Challenged the Normalization of Fracture

On a chilly fall day in 2017, Sally and her husband embarked on a five-hour drive into unknown territory. They were heading to the funeral of their daughter's birth mother. Over the years, they had minimal contact with their daughter's first family. They had never met or spoken to their daughter's first mother, "Jenny," and had spoken only twice to their daughter's first grandmother, "Gwen." The second conversation with Grandmother Gwen occurred after their now-adult daughter instructed them to call Gwen for information on Jenny's funeral arrangements. They talked to Gwen and she invited them to the funeral. A discussion ensued between Sally's husband and herself.

They considered bringing their other two children—who also were adopted—to the funeral. They had concerns about how the children would feel about their own relationships (or lack thereof) with their first families. Would this experience trigger anything in them? Equal to that worry was their concern for their safety. What if their daughter's first family did not really want them there? What if the first family did "something" to them? After a long discussion, they decided to make the journey alone.

Their fears were unfounded. Their daughter's first family welcomed them. Several relatives said they were so grateful to meet Sally and Dan because they had wondered over the past ten years who was caring for their loved one, if she was safe and treated well, and if they were open and kind. Why had it not occurred to them that their daughter's first family would be curious and concerned about the family who had adopted her? Sally and Dan had thought very little about their daughter's beginnings, about the folks who were left behind as they whisked her away to live in their world.

Now, at Jenny's funeral, two worlds were about to overlap. Sally and Dan watched their daughter's first father embrace their daughter in front of the casket as she wept for her first mother. They saw the family, including their daughter, sit together up front—united in their grief.

As the service began their daughter's first father came to sit by Sally and Dan. His act of hospitality became an avenue of connection and a profound gesture of belonging. As Sally sat between two fathers, she began to wonder why on earth she and her husband had not sought, over the years, to nurture more connection between their daughter's first family and themselves—her adoptive family. They had allowed concerns for her safety to avoid seeking healthy ways to be open in the absence of direct interaction.

Because their daughter had spent years in foster care, they made negative assumptions about her first family which led them to fear that their daughter might be hurt or triggered by on-going connection with them. Sally and Dan also feared that they would not become her "full" parents in her mind and feared that she would not assimilate to their ways.

However, there was more behind their lack of effort to stay connected. Sally and Dan were a product of a culture that promotes the fears stated above. They had bought into the cultural belief that a clean break would be better for her.

They were influenced by a culture that has normalized adoption and minimized the fracture of first families as if it is just another way to form a family. However, there was more: it felt safer, simpler, and easier.

Fortunately, much has changed in the past decade. Adoption practice no longer advocates closed adoptions (in most cases) and now encourages open adoption as being less destructive for the child and birth family.

Unfortunately, some adoptive families still choose not to have an on-going connection with their children's birth family before the children are adults. Some adoptive families choose sporadic contact. Some choose minimal contact. Whether by choice or by circumstance, some have little to no knowledge of their child's birth families.

Sally and Dan asked themselves, *How did we wind up so separated from each other?*

Fracture Accepted at the Font

When Sally and Dan carried their children to the baptismal font they felt they understood the power of the sacrament. Their children were now God's children, claimed and named. The Water and the Word also solidified their children's membership in their church family. Not only did they have godparents or sponsors surrounding their children, but also, they had the congregation supporting them. Many people, both figuratively and literally, welcomed their children and embraced them. Their children now belonged.

Sally and Dan failed to consider at the time that their children's first family was both absent and present. They were absent in body, but present in spirit and present within their children.

Dan and Sally had just declared a baptismal welcome. But they overlooked that this welcome extended to every part of their children, including those who gave them life. Unknowingly, they had bought into society's belief that adoption was a fresh start. This fresh start included only the adoptive family, the congregation, and the Triune God. Their belief system made no room for the first family; they were relegated to the past. Indirectly Sally and Dan endorsed and deepened the fracture of the first family by excluding them. Not only were they omitted physically from the elemental action of baptismal belonging, but also, they were spiritually and emotionally deleted. This was a tragedy they came to appreciate only in hindsight.

For many years Sally and Dan did not give much thought to their children's "other" family and felt it quite natural to focus primarily on their adoptive family unit. Yet for Sally and Dan, the funeral of their daughter's first mother challenged their choice to relegate their daughter's family to the back seat of their lives.

A closer look at Scripture reveals that there was nothing natural about this fracture and exclusion. This chapter reconsiders what it means to belong in light of the scriptural foundation for what we call "original belonging."

> *"It was just...all wrong in a way I can't find the words for. Unnatural. Like I'd been zapped into an alternate universe and didn't know how to get home again."* —Jodi H.

Confusion about Cultural and Biblical Adoption

Adoptive children's first lives can be shrouded in mystery and disconnection that has been reinforced by societal and faith-based practices. What faith communities believe about adoption can be traced to how we, The Church as a whole, have interpreted Scripture. From there we have embraced and supported the Western cultural understanding of how the adoption circle is supposed to relate to itself.

David Smolin writes, "...from a legal perspective the Christian adoption movement presumes the kind of adoption which exists in the United States, which in comparative law terms is called full adoption. Full adoption involves a complete legal transference of the child from the original family to the adoptive family, so that after the adoption the child is a legal stranger to their original father, mother, siblings, and all other relatives, while being a full member of the adoptive family. Full adoption generally involves both a new name and a new identity for the child."⁴⁰

Yet, this adoptee points out that,

> *"All of the adoptees in the Bible either know, have contact with, or return to, their birth families."* —*Anonymous*

Indeed, author and law Professor David Smolin, asserts that there is no word for adoption—or an equivalent practice in the Hebrew language or in the Hebrew Scripture. The modern-day adoption construct did not exist. Instead, Jewish law and practices emphasized keeping the lineage and family together.⁴¹

The Orphan and the Widow

A common Christian viewpoint that supports and promotes adoption revolves around our understanding of what the Bible means when it instructs us to care for the orphan and the widow.

One survey respondent raises the issue:

---

⁴⁰ Smolin, David. *Of Orphans and Adoption, Parents and the Poor, Exploitation and Rescue: A Scriptural and Theological Critique of the Evangelical Christian Adoption and Orphan Care Movement.* Samford University, 2012, 3

⁴¹ Smolin, David. Of Orphans and Adoption, Parents and the Poor, Exploitation and Rescue: A Scriptural and Theological Critique of the Evangelical Christian Adoption and Orphan Care Movement. Samford University, 2012,

66 • SCRIPTURAL INTERPRETATION SUPPORTED THE FRACTURE OF FAMILIES •

> *"I did not believe that caring for widows & orphans entailed taking fatherless children from their mothers or orphans from their homeland. I believed that the modern American adoption industry violated more than one of the 10 commandments: don't steal (a child from their family); don't covet (your neighbor's son or daughter because you can't conceive your own); don't lie (on the birth certificate and declare yourself as a parent when you had nothing to do with the child's conception or birth.)"* —Jodi H.

We lift up the phrase: the orphan AND the widow. This conjunction is crucial to how we interpret the command to care for the least of these. In biblical times the word orphan referred to a child who was fatherless. Often an orphan would still have a mother. Before we see orphans and widows as separate, we need to see them as a whole. It is more than possible that the one who is orphaned still has his or her mother.

Since the father was the breadwinner and the inheritor of the family property, if the father died, both the widow and her child had little ability to fend for themselves in the present or the future. Truly this fatherless family unit needed to be cared for and protected. Without the help of the community the orphan and the widow might not have survived.

The desire of faith communities to fulfill the biblical mandate to help widows and orphans must ensure that any child for whom they are seeking adoption is truly an orphan in the contemporary sense. This means the child lacks parents/extended family willing or able to foster or adopt them. Poverty is not a sufficient reason for choosing adoption for a child because it will permanently cut off a child from his ancestral roots, community, culture, or country. This is a high price—one which should not be exacted lightly.

Consider Mother Theresa's words, "The poverty of being unwanted, unloved and uncared for is the greatest poverty."[42] Almost without exception adoptees say that they wrestle with deep, painful feelings of rejection and inadequacy because their birth families chose not to keep them. Regardless of the reasons that precipitated the adoption, the emotion resulting from the fracture of the first family is primal and plagues most adoptees throughout their lives.[43] Adoption plants the seeds of fear that any loving relationship rests on shaky ground and like their birth parents, these people may also relinquish the adoptee out of love.

Adoption must be the last option on any list of solutions, not the first, because it permanently reshapes everyone involved: child, birth parents, and adoptive parents as well as their respective families. That realignment is forever rooted in fracture and should only occur when no alternative remains.

---

[42] https://www.brainyquote.com/quotes/mother_teresa_130839

[43] *Primal Wound: Understanding the Adopted Child*, Nancy Verrier 1993

The best way to fulfill the Great Commission Mandate is to help child and mother remain together.[44] This option not only is more compassionate and is the psychologically and spiritually healthier option.

> *"As to how faith and adoption are meant to work together is that adoption is a last resort that the church should not have anything to do with, that funding works in-country (whether that in-country is your home or abroad) is the best solution, and to imagine how many families could be helped in-country where the tens of thousands of dollars spent on one adoption."* —Sandy B

We also must ensure that the birth family truly understands the complete ramifications of an adoption. This is especially vital in international adoptions. Many cultures have beliefs that significantly differ from the American system of adoption. Some mistakenly think that a child adopted into an American family will return to them in a few years or will send the birth family continuous financial support. Faith communities and adoption facilitators must be scrupulous in clarifying the distinctions about what an adoption will create for the birth family and for the adoptee. It is essential for those who advocate, facilitate, or contemplate an adoption plan for a child to hold this deep appreciation for the realities of adoption.

Dan Cruver offers a comprehensive view that expands our understanding of God's activity in response to those in

---

[44] The Biblical instruction to spread the Word of God throughout the world

need. "The story of the Bible is the story of God visiting us in our affliction, like he once visited Israel (Exo. 4:31), in order to deliver us from it. So, how should this play out with James 1:27? To visit orphans and widows in their affliction means that we work for orphan prevention through family reunification and preservation, and when reunification is not possible, we actively support indigenous adoption efforts. For some children, though, adoption becomes the way we "visit" them."[45]

Modern faith communities can begin to pay attention to the "AND" in the biblical mandate. Before we rush to say that this child truly needs an adoptive home, we can ask, *What about this child's first family?* We can put resources toward finding ways to uplift the "AND" by providing food, shelter, and ways to make a living so that first families can stay together. When we put energy into protection, preservation and prevention, we are honoring the totality of God's call to help the orphan and the widow, as was originally practiced.

Adoption in Christ Jesus, Now Children of God

The New Testament has few, if any, examples of adoption practices. Many Christians will point to Paul's reference to spiritual adoption (Romans 8:15) as a case for the adoption of children. "The Spirit you received does not

---

[45] The First Step in the Way Forward: A Response to David M. Smolin's "Of Orphans and Adoption" By Dan Cruver, page 13. Journal of Christian Legal Thought, Spring 2013

make you slaves, so that you live in fear again; rather, the Spirit you received brought about your adoption to sonship. And by him we cry, "Abba, Father." The Spirit himself testifies with our spirit that we are God's children. Now if we are children, then we are heirs—heirs of God and co-heirs with Christ, if indeed we share in His sufferings in order that we may also share in His glory."

Upon closer examination Paul is using an example of his time to help people understand what a privilege and blessing it is to be called "children of God."

In the Roman Empire if the nobility lacked a male heir, which was required to maintain one's inheritance, a male outside of the family often would be chosen to become a part of the royal fold. Smolin states, "The lack of a suitable heir was thus potentially a great crisis for a significant family, endangering the fundamental purposes of the Roman family...Adoption was thus an accepted solution to the problem of a man lacking a living son who could be his heir...Legally, the adoptee attained a new name and completely new identity, even having all of his debts cancelled, since the prior legal personality ceased to exist. Practically, adopted persons commonly continued their personal relationships with their original family, and even were expected to fulfill some filial duties to their original families. Indeed, since adoption was in legal form often a family to family transaction, it could even be a means of creating alliances between families, similar to the role of marriage in creating alliances between families."[46]

Those who heard Paul's metaphor of adoption would have known that Paul believed that our spiritual adoption is a move upward, a place of honor, an act that assures us of an inheritance we could never have on our own, and a reclaiming of our primary identity as a child of God. After their spiritual adoption by God through baptism Christians still remain in their earthly families and thus retain their connections. *Their identities remain intact.* Paul's audience would have understood this. They most likely would not have equated the metaphor with American-type adoption practices since they usually maintained connection to their original families. Adoption into royalty augmented the original family rather than replaced or diminished it.

Many adoptees have a strong sense that a complete disconnection from their first families is not supported by Scripture. One adoptee expresses this sentiment when he thinks of Joseph and his role in the incarnation.

> *"Growing up, everyone liked to point out to me that Jesus was 'adopted by Joseph' and while that's true (although I'm sure his original OBC was never altered) I always felt envious that he still had his mother."* —Anonymous

When Christians think of the Holy Family Joseph holds a special place in their hearts. He stood by Mary instead of quietly breaking his betrothal to her because of her preg-

---

[46] Smolin, op. cit. 14-15

nancy. Joseph kept their family intact and raised Jesus as his son. Many see this as the model of an adoptive family.

Unlike adoptions in contemporary America, however, Jesus was not separated from his first mother. He and Mary remained together from his birth until his death on the cross. Jesus knew who He was and from whence He came. At the same time, He recognized himself as the Son of God. There was no amended birth certificate, and there were no sealed records.

If not as an adoptive father, how else might we describe Joseph's relationship to Jesus? They lived together as a family; Joseph was the only earthly father Jesus knew. But his relationship with Joseph did not end his relationship with God. We do not hear in Scripture that Joseph ever required Jesus to discontinue his relationship with God or to stop referring to himself as God's Son. In this way Joseph appears to have accepted an expanded definition of family that often has not been supported in secular adoption.

Adult adoptees consistently report that they find it offensive and dismissive when an equivalence is drawn between spiritual adoption by God to the legal adoption of a child. This belief ignores the profound life-long losses adoptees and first families face. While all Christians become God's children through baptism, most remain with the families into which they were born; only adoptees lose their biological families. It follows, therefore, that our spiritual adoption does not mandate or equate with legal adoption.

It is important to lift up quotes from adoptees that reinforce the difficulties that we create when we entwine secular and spiritual adoption. We assert that collapsing secular adoption into spiritual adoption elevates the practice of secular adoption to a higher, spiritual realm where is does not belong. An adoptee responds:

> *"I very much disliked the emphasis on God's "adoption" of believers, because it drew very inaccurate parallels between God's spiritual adoption and the way adoption actually works in the contemporary U.S. U.S. adoption practices don't look anything like the way adoption was practiced in Biblical times." —Rebekah H.*

Only one adoptee respondent found comfort in equating spiritual adoption with his legal adoption.

> *"The NT [New Testament] idea of adopted in Christ resonates strongly." —John H.*

Current cultural beliefs and biblical interpretations have normalized a practice that actually goes against the foundations of God's creative work. By viewing Western adoption as an expression of spiritual adoption, The Church unwittingly has emphasized and reinforced the fracture of families over God's intent to preserve, reconcile, and bring back those who are lost.

In her book *Original Blessing*, Danielle Shroyer speaks about our tendency to focus on brokenness rather than blessedness. "Over the years…we have shifted from telling a story marked by connection to declaring a story marred by distance. And especially in the West, our description of and emphasis on the distance has grown more and more severe."[47]

Aside from specific biblical faith practices and references, God's over-arching behavior stands counter to our current understanding of adoption which imposes a permanent severing of connection to first families.

From the beginning God was intent on restoring and reuniting. The Bible is full of such examples of returning and reconciling. The foundational Christian belief of Christ's death and resurrection provides the greatest testament to God's desire for original belonging. Although many nuanced interpretations of the meaning of Christ's sacrifice exist, all Christians confess that God, out of great love for God's children, sent Christ to save us from fracture and brokenness. The very act of God's Son is an act of bringing us home and recreating belonging.[48]

However, Western thought surrounding adoption has influenced how we perceive adoption and diverted us from God's focus on original belonging. Over time we have heard that if a child is adopted, a permanent break—or at least some time without contact—is better for everyone so that the "new" family can be established. A time of "cocooning" (an intense, temporary period of intimacy as a family unit) is appropriate. Well-meaning

---

[47] The First Step in the Way Forward: A Response to David M. Smolin's "Of Orphans and Adoption" By Dan Cruver, page 13. Journal of Christian Legal Thought, Spring 2013

[48] John 3:16 "For God so loved the world that He gave His only Son, that whoever believes in him shall not perish but have eternal life." NRSV

"outsiders" (friends, colleagues, even extended family) should be held off during the cocooning period immediately after placement. However, this is different from forbidding physical and emotional contact with first families.

Often overlooked is how total isolation or silence affects the child and the birth mother, especially when the wall of silence is permanent.

Professionals tell us that it is important to claim the child as our own. Often, we rename our children and give them names that reflect our (the adoptive parents') lineage and heritage. When a child is old enough to have an awareness of his given name, the loss of this original name would only exacerbate the split in identity and magnify loss. While it is vital that our children have a good sense of belonging with us, it is crucial that they know they belong and fit with their first family as well.

Becky D. writes,

> *"I have always felt connected to the church as a whole on All Saint's Day – the focus on those who came before always brings me peace – peace from the perspective that I am connected with ALL those who came before me. Not just my adoptive family, but my birth family as well. I have always had this vision of all of my ancestors mingling together...There also should not be any shaming around an adoptee's desire to put ALL of the pieces of his/her puzzle together. Adoptive families play an important role. So do birth families."* —Becky D.

We go back to the funeral of Jenny, the first mother of Sally and Dan's daughter. As they drove the five hours on that chilly day, they were anxious, worried, and unsure of what would take place. Would they be welcomed and accepted? Would their daughter call them Mom and Dad when she introduced them and therefore acknowledge their family relationship? Would it be possible for them to all belong together, to be a part of a greater whole? It is striking how their ambivalence and worry about fitting in mirrored what many adoptees feel in their new adoptive homes —a feeling with which many adoptees grapple throughout their lifetimes.

After the funeral Sally and Dan joined the procession to the cemetery and stood with the family as Jenny's body was laid to rest. They heard the words of the pastor who commended Jenny to God's Almighty care. Then they returned to their cars. Their daughter slid into their back seat and accepted their invitation to go out to eat. Then she asked something that Sally and Dan had not even thought to offer, "Can I invite some of my family to join us?" Of course! Why not? Together, at a local restaurant, they broke bread, took pictures, and made connections.

They recalled the warning engrained in them that they would not mesh as an adoptive family if they did not separate themselves from first families. So impressed upon them was this task to make sure that adopted children know that their "true" parents are their adoptive parents that they almost missed the chance to provide their daughter what she truly needed: to be with both of her families.

Yet togetherness, connection, and care are elements of God's original intent, the higher call of God to preserve, unite and reconcile. We, as a church and as adoptive families, can shine the light on not only the biblical mandate for continuity and preservation of family, but also on the necessity for it. For our children we can do no less. They are a part of a first family no matter how known or unknown.

When we retain a part of our children's heritage, either by including a part of their birth names, hanging a picture on the wall of their first mother or family (if available), being open to talking about their first families, or welcoming the first family into our hearts and minds, we validate first families. By doing so, we validate our children.

From the moment we bring our children for dedication or baptism we have an opportunity to witness to an all-inclusive God who desires not brokenness, but connection; togetherness not separation.

An adoptee described her efforts to parse the realities of adoption with her belief in a loving, living God. As you read her words, allow yourself to feel her pain, her struggle, and her hope in God. Pretend you walk in her shoes. Consider her point of view without rebuttal. It grows from the truth of lived experience. She wrote:

> *"When a mother relinquishes her child, the world celebrates this act; however I believe it breaks God's heart and the heart of the child who loses an entire family…But the best part of the sermon was this….even when we make choices that leave God perplexed or broken hearted His response is, 'I can work with that'…Hearing this message helped me to understand that although the world tells me God wanted me adopted and it was "for the best" or "in His perfect plan", I know in my heart, when my mother relinquished me, it broke His heart… He looked at the situation for what it was (broken) and said 'I can work with this mess of a family' and created something beautiful in me in spite of the brokenness. Adoption is not always the answer*

> *to brokenness. Trusting God can bring beauty from the ashes in our lives is what I am discovering...."* —Lynn G.

We cannot and should not seek to negate, replace, or erase first families. For in doing so we would be flying in the face of God's original creation and intent. Just as important, we would be negating a part of our children whom we love.

Instead, we can recognize the source of our fears and address them. We can remind ourselves how our Western ways have distorted adoption and normalized fracture and disruption.

When we take a step back, we make room for first families at the font, in our hearts, in our minds; we honor them in our beliefs, actions, and behaviors. We seek to preserve relationships as much as we possibly can. In doing so, we honor the totality of our beloved children and affirm the right to their beginnings, the right to their original belonging.

Questions to Consider

1. What are your greatest fears around acknowledging and embracing the often-complex relationship with first families?

2. If you are considering adoption, how can you support your child's original belonging?

3. How has this chapter changed your understanding of their relationship with their first family?

4. Adoption is a life-long journey not an event. How does this shift your ideas about adoptees and their relationships with their birth and adoptive families?

Steps to Take

1. Faith communities can respect adoptees' interest in their first families.

2. Reexamine the adoption-related beliefs and theological interpretations which underpin the congregation.

3. Be intentional about modeling respect for the importance of first families to adoptees.

CHAPTER 5

Scripture: Adoptees Heard a Message of Exclusion

All of us read the Bible through the lens of our own experiences. While not every text can be subject to new interpretation, many can be revisited and new understandings may emerge. In this chapter we rethink, reexamine, and realign our understanding of Scripture as it relates to adoptees and their families.

Throughout this book we approach Scripture with a certain framework: our interpretations of Scripture as influenced by our humanity and the context in which we live, and Scripture as inspired by God. Before we read the direct scriptural comments of adoptees it is especially important to understand these basic beliefs. Not only do we have the

SCRIPTURE: ADOPTEES HEARD A MESSAGE OF EXCLUSION

written Word of God to guide us, but also, we have the experience of adoptees and first families who have grappled with Scripture and the interpretation of it by some pastors, theologians, and church members.

Therefore, with all of our humanity, with the love of Christ as our guide, we consider the scriptural views of adoptees, first mothers, and adoptive parents. At the conclusion of this chapter we offer a summary and response to what we have heard.

We compiled the following quotes from the surveys and conversations with adoptees and first mothers.

General Biblical Themes

The Story of Moses (Found in Genesis, Exodus, Leviticus, Numbers, Deuteronomy)

Of all the Scriptures referenced, the story of Moses was mentioned most frequently. One respondent felt that she could relate to Moses as it was told to them; most of the adoptees and first mothers felt differently. For them Moses and his experience may be misrepresented by The Church. Typically, the story is used to exemplify how adoption rescues a child and grafts him or her into a new family and a new life.

Many survey respondents heard the story differently. Rather than a story that affirms adoption, they heard a story that highlighted the ties of original belonging. They notice the persistence of Moses' first mother as she follows her son and becomes his caregiver inside Pharaoh's walls. They lift up Moses' response to his "adoptive" family. As he grows in years, he moves away from his adoptive family and displays his faithfulness to his first family. These adoptees see in the story of Moses the realities of pain, anger, separation, and loss coupled with persistence and strength.

> *"The story of Moses always spoke to me. I felt like he was just like me, looking for his people."* —Sybil E.

> *"Moses' mother nursed him after she relinquished him. This shows me that God values the mother/child relationship and does not desire separation which is the complete opposite of adoption."* —Rebecca F.

> *"All the adoptees in the Bible either know, have contact with, or return to, their birth families. It's challenging to hear everyone talk about Moses being a famous adoptee, but not have them recognize that his natural mother helped raise him or that he eventually returned to "his" people."*
> —Anonymous

> *"A child's mind struggles with being set afloat on a river and abandoned to fate. It is cruel and gives me chills as I write this because it scared me. They could put me in a tiny raft and abandon me at any moment!"* —T. V.

On Solomon, Moses, and Abraham

This respondent sees the damage that can be done to God's original intent when humanity intervenes and makes decisions not for the sake of the child, but for one's own benefit.

> *"Solomon returning the baby to its true mother rather than dividing it between two families. Moses rejecting his adoptive family, returning to his god given family, & then destroying the family & nation that selfishly tried to claim him as their own as though he was a cute little puppy without a family somewhere out there that desperately loved him. Sarah and Abraham going against God's plan and using a handmaiden to adopt a child of their "own." & now our world is STILL at war thanks to the sibling rivalry (& split in the religions) that began with them trying to intervene in God's plan for their family. *eyeroll* Because humans can totally create families more suitable than god himself."* —
> Anonymous

Specific Biblical Texts

Numbers 14:18 "The Lord is slow to anger, and abounding in steadfast love, forgiving iniquity and transgression, but by no means clearing the guilty, visiting the iniquity of the parents upon the children to the third and the fourth generation."

The idea that God curses children for the sins of their father leaves many people uncomfortable. It contradicts their belief in a "fair" and loving God. Science—specifically epigenetics[49]—offers us a way to interpret this generational effect not as a divine punishment but rather as the logical result of human decisions and the chaotic and traumatic circumstances they set in place.

Dr. Gabor Maté speaks of the impact of a surrendering mother's prenatal stress.[50] Parental state at conception and prenatal environment both influence the developing fetus. It creates a physiology of abandonment and affects the unborn child in profound ways that change neural architecture, hormonal set points, and creates a channel for communicating transgenerational trauma.[51] The field of Epigenetic studies the process of intergenerational changes and how these shifts directly affect functioning in subsequent offspring. Biological Psychiatry: A Journal of Psychiatric Neuroscience and Therapeutics has published many articles on the process. Research reveals that children indeed suffer the consequences of the previous generations. Their biology imposes the sentence.

> *"Why was I relinquished? 'Your sins are visited upon you through your children.' I often thought it was punishment for my parents' sins!"* —Lorraine R.

---

[49] Experience-Dependent Epigenetic Modifications in the Central Nervous System https://www.biologicalpsychiatryjournal.com/article/S0006-3223(08)01319-X/fulltext

[50] Maté, Dr. Gabor. Never Too Late: Addressing the Long-Term Effects of Childhood Trauma , Sounds True, Healing Trauma Summit, June 4, 2018

> *"I was told I was a child of sin; their bio children were children of love. I was always understanding of my position as a bastard, a lesser person not worthy of god [sic]. To be quite honest, I don't want anything to do with a god that blames a child for the sins of the parents, and will continue to do so for 10 generations."* —Ann W.

Deuteronomy 23:2 "A bastard shall not enter into the congregation of the LORD; even to his tenth generation shall he not enter into the congregation of the LORD."[52]

The harsh language and consequences of Deuteronomy will trouble many who seek to be faithful to the text as it is printed. Without the context of this writing, The Church can shame some adoptees because of the circumstances surrounding their first family. Adopted children sometimes find themselves unwelcome in some churches that believe the stain of bastardy taints their status without some act of cleansing or rebirth. The overarching love of God in Christ Jesus eclipses the legalistic nature of this text. These respondents felt the shaming that this literal reading might create.

> *"I have even had that quoted to me and heard it in a sermon when I attended a fundamentalist Church. And there are still church-goers today who take the Bible literally and believe this, and they are the ones I take issue with. We as adoptees cannot help the circumstances of our births and certainly should not be forced to defend them. Yet I have found myself doing just that."* —Nicole B.

---

[52] https://www.kingjamesbibleonline.org/Deuteronomy-23-2/

> *"Failing to recognize that, by choosing an unmarried woman to be the mother of Jesus, God showed us that being an unmarried mother is not justification for the Church to scorn unmarried mothers."* —S. Morris

The Psalms

The two Psalms referenced below can bring great comfort to people, including children who are searching for their identity and place in life. To know that you are God's creation and God's child, wonderfully made, can assure children that they were not a mistake as this adoptee expresses:

> *"Since I was conceived as a result of a rape, I thought I was a mistake. Now I see that I can't be a mistake if I'm God's child and wonderfully made."* —Anonymous

However, in a later chapter we will speak about the use of the word "gift" when speaking about children who are adopted and the pressure this can create for children. Even more, these scriptures can highlight the conflict of being born to one woman and placed with another.

Psalm 139

SCRIPTURE: ADOPTEES HEARD A MESSAGE OF EXCLUSION

> *"I actually have aversions to Psalm 139, when I read it and think about God knitting me together in my mother's womb... I wonder why I ended up where I did."*
> —Anonymous

Psalm 127:3 "Behold, children are a gift of the Lord, the fruit of the womb is a reward."

> *"When did it become acceptable to give away our family? We don't give away family members. We just don't. And, contrary to the pro-life argument, adoption isn't the alternative to abortion, parenting is."* —Stephanie M.[53]

Mark 8:29 "But who would you say that I am?"

Jesus poses this question to his disciples who have heard conflicting reports of Jesus' identity. They were unsure of this man they were following. As he does often when questioned, Jesus requires the disciples to think for themselves and discover Jesus' identity. This brief exchange between Jesus and his disciples may mirror not only our own questions of who Jesus is, but also questions of who we are as people of God or individuals. When this adoptee reads this verse, the search for identity is reflected.

> *"I thought about this a lot as a teenage adoptee who had no clue about myself."* —Paige S.

---

[53] https://bleedingheartsadoption.wordpress.com/2017/07/04/the-church-and-adoption-changing-the-narrative/

Luke 15: 11-32 The Parable of the Lost Son

Many of us have learned this parable in Sunday school and heard it preached in the pulpit. Each time we may hear different parts of the story in new ways: the son who squanders his inheritance, the jealousy of the faithful son who remains and does what his father asks, and the father who celebrates the son's return. This former foster child who had a difficult relationship with her first family shares how she receives this story. It may surprise us:

> *"The prodigal son story makes me sad. When I hear it, I wonder if my first family would celebrate my return the way the father did for his son."* —Lolita

While the following quote does not directly reference the prodigal son parable, it expresses the palpable need to be welcomed and claimed. For this adoptee the experience of being worthy of belonging transformed her.

> *"I remember being at Bible camp that summer after my 15th birthday, when I became a Christian... I remember sitting on the beach late at night and listening to the staff do worship music. One song had the lyrics, "He's coming back to claim his own." That hit me in a place that I didn't know existed. Nobody had ever come back for me. Not my dad or my mom or my siblings or anyone... If God wanted to call me his own and come back for me, I'd go with Him."*
> —Jodi H.

Equally worth telling are her subsequent thoughts which reveal how her initial sense of welcome and belonging crashed. She had drawn a false equivalence between her spiritual belonging and her expectation that it could rescind her adoption. This is an example of the danger of equating spiritual and legal adoption.

> *"I think I had hoped becoming a Christian would make up for the earthly family I didn't have ... I felt let down after I realized God, or God's people weren't going to take me away from the adopters and give me a new life somewhere ... where I could safely be myself. It didn't happen. And that's when I became suicidal."—Jodi H.*

James 1:27 "Religion that God our Father accepts as pure and faultless is this: to look after the orphans and widows in their distress and to keep oneself from being polluted by the world."[54]

Above we read from the book of James which often is cited as the book that describes our faith in action. Christians pay special attention to what James offers as ways we can make our faith alive with the works we perform in this life. Many seek to pattern their life and their decisions on what they read in James. These adoptees challenge Christians to consider the context of the time, our current culture, and the pressing needs of our world as they seek to live out their faith.

This verse from James often is cited as a command to adopt. This adoptee has other thoughts for what The Church should be supporting:

> *"I have seen this wave of Christians decide that adoption is what they're called to do. White Saviors. And, The Church gets behind them, including financial support. Do we see*

---

[54] https://www.kingjamesbibleonline.org/James-1-27/

the conflict? Do we understand that the majority of the time a mother is considering adoption it's simply because she's lacking support and resources? Yet, we will rally around these families in their quest to "bring their children home." Why are so many church members spending tens of thousands of dollars to remove a child from their family and their culture when that money could be used to BUILD SOMETHING; a safe place for them to remain together in the countries that have poverty and deep cultural stigma? Why aren't we helping by keeping their family intact, rather than removing their children? Why isn't this ministry within The Church? Why aren't we preserving families first? How have so many people, seemingly, misinterpreted and misconstrued the meaning of this verse? What would Jesus do?" —Stephanie M.

1 Peter 4:8 "Above all, love each other deeply because love covers over a multitude of sins."

When an expectant mother comes to a church for support, our response should be one of love and not judgment. Love should guide the way to her need. This first mother hopes for love to win out in our response to and care of first mothers.

"In the last few years I have had the opportunity to get to know other mothers and hear their adoption stories. The same thread runs through many of their experiences, which is, that the news of the pregnancy was met with shame and despair by not only family but members of their church. Shame? It's a baby, a new life. Perhaps if we alter our responses to unplanned pregnancy from the shame game to what it really is, a precious gift—a gift for your family, not someone else's – the stigma attached will begin to fade. Pregnancy isn't a sin. Motherhood isn't a sin. A baby isn't a sin."[55]

---

[55] The Church and Adoption: Changing the Narrative. https://bleedingheartsadoption.wordpress.com/2017/07/04/the-church-and-adoption-changing-the-narrative/

SCRIPTURE: ADOPTEES HEARD A MESSAGE OF EXCLUSION

Life experiences—especially those as life altering and profound as adoption—bring a layer of understanding and complexity to biblical stories, beliefs, and commands. The comments of adoptees and first mothers reveal that Scripture resonates strongly with them, sometimes in ways that run counter to our presuppositions. Adoption creates a filter of heightened awareness of, and raw sensitivity to, these texts and how they are used throughout the life of The Church. As we have seen from the quotes above, adoptees and first mothers call for an awakened response of empathy, education, and a broader viewpoint of Scripture.

Questions to Consider:

1. How do these reflections challenge your own interpretation of these texts?

2. How can congregations, pastors, and Sunday school teachers include the views of adoptees when they read these texts or stories?

3. Mary and Jesus remained together when Joseph became Jesus' earthly father. How does this example differ from current adoption practice?

Steps to Take:

1. Consider an adoptee's possible point of view when reading Scripture. Put yourself in his/her shoes.

2. When sharing these powerful texts and stories with others lift up the complexity of Scripture and invite comments that wrestle with the text as understood and written.

3. How does this chapter expand or change your ideas about the connection between Scripture and adoption?

Chapter 6

Listen, Learn, and Lean in with Empathy

Now that we have taken an honest look at our cultural practices, examined foundational beliefs, and considered new understandings of Scripture, we are poised to look at what The Church can do differently. Adoptees and first families have spoken and we are listening. Let's revisit the words of adult adoptees who told us they want—need—the church to support them with understanding and acceptance. We feel the weight of their suffering on our hearts and want to answer the call to serve in ways that are helpful, respectful, and adequately informed. Pastors and church members do not magically possess the Adoption-attuned awareness we recommend. It has to be learned. Otherwise old patterns, unexamined beliefs, assumptions, and actions will remain unchanged and adoptees and first families will continue to struggle.

Hear one adoptee's wish:

> *"Could we require pastors to receive adoption training?"*
> —*Lynn G.*

Empathize with First Families and Adoptees

Thousands of children were separated from their families during the Holocaust like Gabor Maté, who was taken from his mother at the tender age of one. He personally experienced maternal/child separation and understands viscerally how it shapes a child. Regardless of the cause of the separation—war, illness, death, adoption—the impact is profound and painful.

This seminal experience fueled his interest in healing trauma. The effects of his separation from his mother continue to influence and challenge him today. Dr. Gabor Maté became a physician who specializes in healing addiction and trauma. He asserts, "Only when compassion is present will people allow themselves to see the truth." [56] This lens of compassion opens a pathway that is useful for dealing with adoption complexity for both the adoptee and those around him. Empathy and compassion open our eyes to things to which we might otherwise remain blinded be-

---

[56] Maté, Dr. Gabor. Never Too Late: Addressing the Long-Term Effects of Childhood Trauma, Sounds True, Healing Trauma Summit, June 4, 2018

cause they challenge our expectations and beliefs of what is or can be true.

Adoption-attunement asks us to examine our beliefs and actions regarding adoption, to move beyond the boundaries of presuppositions and assumptions that obscure previously unseen truths. Recall the elements of AQ:

- Consider grief and loss issues
- Use sound adoption language
- Understand the attachment process
- Respect birth parents and first families
- Model, teach, and hold healthy boundaries
- Educate family, friends, teachers, and faith communities on adoption
- Remember a child's story belongs to him
- Recognize adoption as a family experience
- Encourage playfulness and good humor as a family value
- Integrate child's birth heritage
- Honor child's need to know and connect with birth family
- Nurture and value child's innate talents, encourage them to be themselves
- Recognize parents must work through their own grief and loss issues
- Follow ethical practices
- Operate with a child-centric focus

Adoption-attunement resets both the heart and mind. It requires us to use all of our intellect. When we mention intelligence most of us think about IQ. Other types of intelligence also exist and will serve our mission. We must draw on our IQ, AQ (Adoption-attunement Intelligence), and EQ (Emotional Intelligence.)[57] To bring authentic and revolutionary empathy to our adoption-connected relationships, we need all of these intelligences. We also must be grounded in our Spiritual Intelligence: the Christian belief that all people are children of God.

Embracing this level of sensitivity and understanding is far more comprehensive than simply reading words on a list. Each element requires us to shift our approach and to respond with empathy, intentionality, and commitment. Empathy exceeds simple awareness of adoption complexity; it acknowledges, validates, and accepts without minimizing. When we follow these elements, we serve members of the adoption constellation in a better way. Let's examine each AQ element in detail.

Share the Knowledge

Because of the deeply entrenched belief that adoption is divinely ordained, it is important to restate that Adoption-attunement asserts family preservation is more aligned with God's desire for his children. Keeping families intact does not contradict or contravene divine will, rather, it outlines a pathway that aligns and better fulfills it with compassion and an awareness of innate human needs. Now that we

---

[57] Dr. Daniel Goleman, Ph.D., "Emotional Intelligence: Why It Can Matter More Than IQ", Bantam Books, 2005

have learned this, we do not keep this knowledge to ourselves under a proverbial basket. As admonished in Matthew 5:16,[58] we choose to share the light of our adoption-attuned knowledge so that it gives light unto all. Now that we know better, not only *can* we do better, but also, we *must* do better.

This knowledge obliges us to teach the benefits of Adoption-attunement to as many people as we can. Armed with this information we can spread the light and advance the healing process. Just as Simon of Cyrene helped Jesus carry His cross, we also have a part to play in alleviating the suffering of adoptees and their families. We cannot take away their personal crosses but we can help with the heavy lifting.

Consider Grief and Loss Issues

To consider grief and loss issues means we engage in conversations about the various elements of Adoption-attunement. More significantly, we welcome them. This helps us learn what adoptees truly need—as distinct from what we *think* they need. We discover how they *actually* feel versus how we think they ought to feel. We accept that adoption is not a Hallmark© card experience. This is a significant distinction because conversations about adoption complexity may prove difficult, uncomfortable, and even challenging. Still we must embrace this dialog if we truly want to serve and support adoptees and their families.

---

[58] King James, 2000

We know it is possible to nurture the healing and wholeness which God desires for his people. We recognize that each of us is called to bring it forth. Healer Leslie Booker calls this "embodying radical presence."[59] To accomplish this, faith communities will want to set aside idealized, traditional notions and expectations about adoption and bear witness to the realities of the adoptee experience. This commitment to truth and love is an integral part of the Christian faith.

Adoptees and first parents yearn to have their grief and loss issues acknowledged. They do not want to be told that they should be grateful, consider themselves lucky not to have been aborted, or be expected to pretend that everything is fine, or that they should be happy because they (or their child) got "new and better" parents in the deal. An adoptee pleads:

> *"Do not make the adoptee feel... ungrateful in any way, or suggest that he or she has done anything wrong by searching for his or her birth family. We have a right to our heritage and our story."* —Nicole B.

When adoptees are only "allowed" to mention the benefits of adoption, no space exists for the total reality of the adoptee's experience. Benefits do not erase the pain. The truth is that any adoption-connected gains co-exist with the inherent losses. Adoptees want their entire experience to be

---

[59] Leslie Booker, The Healing Trauma Summit, Interview with Dr. Jeffrey Rutstein. *"Embodying Radical Presence: Awareness of Race, Culture, and Self in Healing Trauma"*

"seen." Whitewashing their grief and loss or expecting them to be grateful for these losses and secrets as the "cost" of joining their adoptive families turns a blind eye to the genuine pain and generations-long losses which adoptees and first families experience. It is unrealistic and unfair to expect these attitudes.

> *"I tried to close that big black hole of my heritage and medical records ... the ambivalence with which I was dealing when I found them and tried to wrestle with nature vs. nurture."* —Carla B.

On the eve of his betrayal Jesus prayed for his disciples to witness his agony in the Garden of Gethsemane. Adoptees also pray for witnesses to their suffering. They need and desire us to encourage conversations about their real, lived experiences, not just tolerate them. Requiring silence is not an option; it is a soul-crushing blow. We must respond to Jesus' call to stay awake to suffering.

When church families offer genuine empathy instead of dismissal, adoptees feel seen, heard, and supported. This kind of connectivity is the embodiment of Christian service and love. Faith communities can be conduits of God's love and the healing and sense of belonging that adoptees seek. Instead of feeling invalidated and unseen in faith communities, adoptees and first parents can find the safe harbor they need and, in the process, draw closer to God.

Faith communities will want to end the "Yes, but…" conversations that acknowledge only the gains of adoption and instead listen, bear witness, and offer compassion. Jesus understood the cross was His to bear. Still he yearned for His disciples to watch and witness His suffering. Adoptees and first parents call us to this same act of compassion and acknowledgment. An adoptee suggests one way faith communities can better address the adoptee experience:

> *"By accepting and promoting honesty for anything the adoptee says/shares and wishes to know. Same for adoptive parents and social work professional involved."* —Paige S.

Once we understand and embrace these concepts, we will have truly increased our AQ. We can then blend this intelligence with our intellectual and emotional intelligences and bring a full-hearted approach to our response to adoptees and their families.

> *"Up until the last couple of years, it [church] was terrible. I always felt judged and looked down upon. Now I have a great church family behind me."* —Anonymous

Don't "Should" on Adoptees

Once adoption has occurred, what do adoptees and their families—first and adoptive—seek the most? They hunger for empathy, validation, and support. They do not want others to try to fix their issues, problems, or challenges, but they do want people to believe and acknowledge that those challenges exist. They need access to adequate resources so they can overcome their circumstances. They definitely do not want outsiders (those who are not directly part of an adoption) telling them how they should think or feel. In short, they need an Adoption-attuned response.

Too often people presume to advise or lecture adoptees about how they should feel about being adopted, that they should express gratitude to their parents, and that they should feel lucky to have those parents. Unless one has been invited to offer guidance on the subject and one is trained to understand and counsel adoptees, only one response is appropriate: to offer a listening ear, an empathetic heart, and hands willing to provide whatever support they have requested. Ratchet down the expectations, the judgments, the advice, and the criticism.

Most of all, do not "should" on adoptees. Avoid dismissive platitudes. Remember Jesus' words in Gethsemane, "My soul is deeply grieved, to the point of death; remain here and keep watch with me."[60] Jesus knew the apostles could not take away His cup, but He needed them to observe and acknowledge His suffering. This is precisely what adoptees ask of us. They seek the grace of compassionate witness.

Imagine being on the receiving end of such unsolicited and uninformed advice on a deeply personal issue. No one offers similar guidance to people raised by their biological parents; yet they also have been blessed—with parents who didn't abort them or give them away, and instead raised and loved them. Given the option, most people would prefer to

---

[60] Matthew 26:36-46 New American Standard Bible (NASB)

stay with the parents who created them. From the vantage point of being "kept" or being "surrendered" the lucky ones are those who remain safely in their intact family of origin.

> *"Adult adoptees aren't children, and we're made to feel like children when you ask questions like how do your parents feel about you finding your birth family."* —Lisa F.

Validate the Full Spectrum of Adoption Experience

Raise awareness of how adoption is discussed in sermons. Neither glorify nor oversimplify adoption. Present it in its totality—the gains and losses, the duality, and the complexity. Propose a range of solutions to help mothers struggling to raise their children, and include adoption as only one possibility—and not the first or the only option offered. Endorse adoptees' rights to have relationships with both of their families.

Provide Emotional Sanctuary

Adoptees plead for faith communities to channel God's ability to restore and heal by being the safe harbor they need. They yearn for validation instead of minimization and dismissiveness, for understanding instead of unsolicited advice, for privacy instead of intrusive curiosity. Until they experience this level of acceptance and security, they will be unable to trust that it is safe for them to be vulnerable and honest.

"The church needs to be a place of understanding—a sanctuary community—a place of protection where adoptees can feel free to share their story without fear of being labeled 'ungrateful.'" —Carla B.

Offer Counsel through an Adoption-attuned Lens

Pastors and other faith leaders can play a vital role in the emotional and spiritual well-being of adoptees and their families when they offer a compassionate and supportive presence that focuses on careful listening, validating, reflecting, and empathizing. This open and non-judgmental approach can reinforce God's love for the person seeking counsel.

Be Mindful of Unintended Consequences

As we have stated throughout this book, good intentions offer a good start. However, good intentions alone are not enough. Even the best intentions can create some unintended consequences. Thus, we must ensure that our methods accomplish the intended purpose, and do not, in fact, make situations worse. In her landmark book, *The Child Catchers*, Kathryn Joyce quotes UNICEF's Doug Webb: "'If you build an orphanage, it will be filled…Children who were not homeless or unparented before end up becoming institutionalized as a direct result of orphanages setting up shop in poor areas."[61] Consider the recent position advocated by the United Nations. "Today, for the first time ever, all 193 member states of the United Nations have formally recognised that orphanages don't protect children, they harm them, and have called for the progressive elimination of institutional care globally."[62]

Children who become adopted transnationally experience grave losses, even if they join families where their standard of living is improved. Yes, they gain a family; they also lose a family, and a culture, and a language, and a country. Of course, we want to support widows and orphans, but we do not want to create orphans. The best way to support widows and orphans is to keep them together, not tear them apart unless there is truly no other safe alternative.

> *"Faith leaders need to back away from the hyper-adoption focus and widen their humanitarian views to find creative ways to support communities in need."* —Rebekah H.

Infuse Homilies and Rituals with Compassion

When talking about topics like motherhood keep in mind the variety of people fulfilling the role: step-parents, foster parents, grand-parents serving as parents, parents

---

[61] Joyce, Kathryn. The Child Catchers: Rescue, Trafficking and the New Gospel of Adoption, Public Affairs, 2013

[62] hopeandhomes.org/news-article/unga/?fbclid=IwAR00tAA8CC Qt6LyoOduWdLNR6HID03UMO9C7jpUiSSxIIglTKdNQDqSbuhQ

whose children have died, birth parents who lost their children to adoption, etc., as well as women struggling with infertility or the death of a child. Choose an inclusive lens that recognizes the complexity of parenting.

Understand the Attachment Process

Attachment occurs over time through repeated interactions in which a child expresses a need and a parent responds successfully. Like a game of relationship tennis, it involves both serve and return. Sometimes connection occurs; sometimes the serve or the return strays wildly. The goal is to keep the interaction going, alternately serving and returning. For healthy attachment to occur, accurate relationship responses must significantly outnumber misses.

No handbook exists that guarantees connection, but trust and honesty are essential. Every relationship is unique; some have more baggage that must be unpacked, refolded, and prioritized. One hundred-percent accuracy is impossible. Successful attachment is a long-term result that does not occur in a linear fashion. No mathematical formula outlines how many interactions will produce the desired closeness.

To successfully build attachment the child must feel heard, seen, validated, and valued. Every fractured parental relationship—separation from a first mother, foster parent, etc.—that a child suffers chips away at her confidence that relationships will be permanent and that it is safe to reciprocate and attach. The severing of significant parent-figure relationships makes the establishment of successor relationships more complicated and more risky and can have devastating consequences.

> *"I was an outsider in my church as well as in my own family."* —Julie G.

Errors will occur, some forced and some unforced. Whenever breakdown occurs repair must follow promptly. Heartfelt apologies must be proffered and—ideally—accepted. Both parent and child will need to offer and receive forgiveness. The best way to teach forgiveness is by modeling it. Genuine apologies include a firm resolve to do better along with a commitment to not repeat the

mistake. Over time, trust increases and the seeds of loving attachment sprout.

Faith communities that understand this complex process can offer better counsel and guidance to adoptive parents who struggle to navigate the attachment process with their child. Parents can become discouraged and even filled with despair and fear when attachment fails to build with the speed and depth they earnestly desire and expect. The attachment process can be quite lengthy and weighed down by behaviors that intentionally fend off connection. Volumes have been written on this topic. For kids who experienced trauma, relationship reciprocity is often scant and sometimes non-existent for long periods of time. This can prove very challenging and discouraging for the parents.

Some reasons adoptees resist attachment are unconscious and defensive: since their first families chose not to parent them—regardless of the reasons—they experienced rejection. Thus, they may withhold themselves to prevent a repeat of parental rejection. Some children take a more aggressive approach. They engage in I'll-hurt-you-before-you-can-hurt-me types of behavior. (Behavior is the language of trauma, especially preverbal trauma.) This lose/lose strategy hurts child and parent. However, because it arises out of the child's primal need for self-preservation, it is difficult for him or her to risk trying a new strategy, especially one that leaves them vulnerable and exposed.

Yet another way of looking at this is: the adoptee rejects the adoptive parent, thus creating a sad repetition of the rejection process from a position which the child controls. With any of these strategies, tragically, the adoptee delays or loses out entirely on the possibility of creating a healing and reassuring relationship bond. Many adoptees both crave and fear attachment. They yearn to belong yet hesitate to expose themselves to the risk of additional rejection.

This deeply grieves parent and child. Both are reeling from the pain of their circumstances.[63] The parent mourns the resistance of a deeply desired, healthy, and joyous connection to a child; the child mourns the security of an uninterrupted and safe relationship with the parents who created him. Looking to assign blame or find fault helps no one. They all need empathy and comfort. It is when traumatized children behave in the most unreasonable and unlikeable ways that they are most sorely in need of love and accep-

---

[63] Schooler, Jane et al. Wounded Children Healing Homes: How Traumatized Children Impact Adoptive and Foster Families, NavPress

tance. Given their history, their distancing behavior is an understandable, although self-defeating strategy.

This type of defensive attachment strategy is often called "RAD" or Reactive Attachment Disorder. We prefer to think of it as a logical—although counter-productive—strategy in the face of their having suffered previous emotional assaults on the safe "serve and return" process of healthy attachment building.

Parents need endless persistence and hope in the face of a child's repeated rebuffs. In such circumstances they may turn to a faith community for comfort and guidance. It is important that all counselors understand attachment complexity.[64] This will ensure that the child's behavior will not be misconstrued or mislabeled as defiant, ungrateful, or contradictory to God's will. Instead it will be seen as the child's trauma response, one which cannot be disciplined away or cured with love alone, but which can be addressed with love, faith, Adoption-attuned competence, and Christian hope. And time. Lots and lots of time.

Every fracture of primal relationships exacts a significant toll on the child's willingness and ability to risk future attachments. Any subsequent fracture magnifies the damage, increases distrust, and scars the child. Marshall every effort to avoid additional separations. Provide adoptive and foster families support and interventions that nurture relationships so they don't fall apart.

---

[64] Ziegler, Ph.D., Dave, Traumatic Experience and the Brain: A Handbook for Understanding and Treating Those Traumatized as Children, Phoenix, Acacia Publishing. 2002

Respects Birth Parents and First Families

Once Christians embrace Adoption-attunement, it infuses ministries with an ability to recognize the adoption complexity that had been previously invisible. The traditional point of view from which counsel and advice emanated tended to be primarily adoptive-parent focused. Adopters were lauded as rescuers who were doing the Lord's work by accepting another's child as one of their own. Their "generous, selflessness" saved the birth mother—and her family—from the "shame" of an unplanned pregnancy (or the "sin" of one out of wedlock), and simultaneously provided a family to a child in need of one. This overly-simplistic viewpoint made no room for the grief and loss of the first parents and the child for whom adoption was contemplated.

While the traditional view of adoption cast the child as The Big Winner, it ignored the obvious—yet significant—fact: the adopting parents received a huge benefit, too. They secure the opportunity to create and enjoy a parent/child relationship. Adoption also relieves and rescues many adopters from the pain and stigma of childlessness.

The world shared the adoptive family's genuine joy of welcoming a baby (or older child) yet seemed blind to the first parents' anguish and the complex burden that adoption would place on the child's life. Faith communities have a broader mission to minister to all people affected by an adoption. This includes first parents, their extended families, and also the extended families of the adopting parents. We can stand as witnesses to the totality of the experience and lay aside judgment and shaming. Jean S. points out that

> *"Jesus mother was unmarried when she got pregnant, just like my mother."* —Jean S.

Joseph did not send Mary away; he stood by her. Similarly, faith communities can stand by women facing unplanned pregnancy. Churches can maintain a catalog of resources that a mother can access so that she and her child can remain together. Many women would choose to parent if they only had access to reliable and sustained assistance. This includes: child care, transportation, housing, shelter, and health care as well as a support person to call in moments of unplanned emergencies. We must never lose sight that adoption is a very permanent, generations-long solution to what are usually temporary problems.

A crisis pregnancy overwhelms an expectant mother emotionally and physically. It can easily compromise her ability to identify and marshal the resources she needs. Faith communities can rally around these mothers and their children and be the linchpin that keeps a family intact. They can keep a registry of social service agencies and the type of assistance that communities offer; train mentors who can walk women through the labyrinth of service agencies; and offer new ministries like: foster grandparents, child care, clothing, baby equipment, toy exchanges, and transportation, etc.

Lynn Grubb, President of Adoptees Rights Coalition suggests these ways in which people can support expectant mothers, adoptive and foster families.

- Parent a child while your relative/close friend gets back on his or her feet.
- Become a mentor to kids in your community.
- Become a CASA/Guardian ad Litem in your community.
- Support non-profits like the Adoptee Rights Coalition and Adoption Network Cleveland that do legislative work.
- Support non-profits that have active support groups such as Adoptees Connect.
- Support your local kinship program or develop one such as Ali Caliendo did in Las Vegas.
- Provide respite for foster parents formally or informally.
- Do a church fundraiser for foster kids so they can have proper luggage or bags to transport their items (instead of black garbage bags).
- Support a family at Christmas and provide gifts.
- Support family preservation groups such as **FP365** and **Saving Our Sisters**.

Some women still will decide to make an adoption plan and they will need emotional and spiritual support to address their complex feelings surrounding their decision. Their need will spiral throughout their lives. Birth grandparents also will be deeply affected by the loss of this child. Concentrate on meeting their lifetime-support needs. Faith communities can be the face of God through compassion and understanding and leave any judgment to God.

Questions to Consider

1. As a faith community, how does Adoption-attunement redefine your understanding of the benefits of adoption as well as the coexistence of loss and gain after adoption?
2. How have relationship fractures in your own life affected your inclination to trust others?
3. How does your experience of broken trust influence your ability to empathize with adoptees?

Steps to Take

1. Follow the Golden Rule when counseling expectant mothers and adoptees.
2. Become clear on the genuine losses which adoption creates.
3. Embrace the elements of Adoption-attunement (AQ) and share it with the congregation.

CHAPTER 7

What Parents and Families Can Do

Educate Family, Friends, Teachers, and Faith Communities on Adoption

This book examines the myths, outdated cultural assumptions, and misinformation surrounding adoption. These fictions have failed the people they purported to serve. Now that we know better, we have the opportunity—the obligation—to do better. We believe this is also true in the adoption arena. That is why all who are awakened to Adoption-attunement will want to share their knowledge whenever and wherever possible. It will help parents be better parents, counselors be more effective, and faith communities and schools be more supportive.

Adoption strives to be a positive solution. We now realize it also generates many unintended consequences for which people were unprepared. The rose-colored glasses of cultural assumption leave no room for the existence of very real fallout. Adoption is an imperfect solution which parents and children do not walk through unscathed. Painting it as a win/win/win devastates lives, builds walls, and alienates people from their faith communities—a very unintended and undesired consequence.

A hyper-positive cultural viewpoint clouds reality and undermines adoptees, first parents, and even adoptive parents. Boxed in by myths, ill-informed guidance, and expectations adoptees and their families (birth and adoptive) have floundered. Most have been operating on a blueprint that did not fit.

When adoptees and their families collapsed under the weight of their struggles, they sought counsel. Often, they found the professionals to whom they turned lacked adoption-competency and adoption-attunement. This must change. Too many people have missed a chance to genuinely serve adoptees. To be effective anyone providing support must bring education, empathy, and an accurate understanding of adoption complexity. In other words, they must operate from an Adoption-attuned perspective. AQ recognizes the challenges, trauma and conflicts, and seeks to walk with adoptees as they navigate their lives and strive to find healing and wholeness. Imagine how Jesus would want us to approach families in crisis. We assert that He would embrace compassion, truth—the core of Adoption-attunement—and would work to hold families together. Jesus would eschew secrecy, lies, coercion, condemnation and a predisposition to dividing families. He would love and enfold them and assure them that they belong.

> *"Allow [adoptees] the freedom to grieve [adoption] as a true loss of losing a loved one."* —*Anonymous*

Remember a Child's Story Belongs to the Child

Our culture thirsts for gossip and a peek into other's private lives. People feel free—even entitled—to know information that is actually none of their business. Adoptees and their families encounter such boundary assaults constantly. Sometimes they are blatant: *How much did Rosa cost?* Other times breaches happen gradually via a sequence of questions that become more and more invasive. *Was her birth mother young? Did she abuse drugs? Does she even know who the father is?* Such privacy violations serve no useful purpose and leave adoptive families shell-shocked.

Thrilled by the arrival of their child, adoptive parents are eager to share their joy. They want their extended families and communities to welcome their child so they tend to view people's questions as innocent. In their eagerness to engender empathy, parents may be tempted to share details of the trauma, abuse, or difficult circumstances which led to their child's adoption.

But this information belongs to the child. Parents have no right to share it. Other people should not learn this information before the child does. Imagine having the details of your private life being aired for everyone to know—everyone except you. Consider how it might affect the way people view you now and in the future. Pretend that the information being sought is *your* information. Would you want other people to know it? Would sharing it with others support you? Or, would it embarrass or compromise you?

Whether it is friends, family, or faith community, there is virtually no reason to share the specific details of a child's story with anyone except professionals actively treating the child. What is appropriate to share with outsiders? Parents can share generalities: *His birth mother faced over-whelming circumstances,* or: *Nathan experienced significant trauma from which we are helping him heal.* This level of sharing preserves a child's privacy and still allows people to know that he endured tough stuff for which he needs their compassion, patience, and support.

Motive and context are important for both questioners and respondents. Before posing a question to an adoptee, adoptive, or first parent, consider if you would feel comfortable answering the question if it were posed to you and about you. Identify the purpose driving the question. Mere curiosity is insufficient! Questioners should secure permission and ensure that the time and place are conducive to a personal conversation. Anything people are willing to share is a gift and an act of trust that deserves respect.

Another adoptee describes her perspective on these "interrogations." She emphasizes the importance of being able to control the conversation.

> *"As long as it's on my terms, I share to inform and educate as much as I can."* —Casey S.

Parents who receive questions about their child's adoption story hold two important objectives. First, ensure that their child receives the support and empathy regarding his challenges while always preserving their child's right to privacy. Second, educate others on how to understand adoption complexity.

Recognize Adoption as a Family Experience

Perhaps this header left you thinking this statement is blatantly obvious. Of course it is a family experience because adoption provides a family to a child in need of one. But this aspect of Adoption-attunement includes many layers. Adoption is not something which happens only to the adoptee. Every member of the adoption constellation experiences a permanent realignment of their life-trajectory and relationships. Adoption reshapes each of them and places their lives on a new course with new people with whom to share it. At every stage of life adoption will be one of the influences that affect them emotionally, intellectually, physically, and spiritually. It will influence the way they think of themselves, sustain relationships, and perceive God's role in their lives.

Encourage Playfulness and Good Humor as a Church and a Family Value

The importance of playfulness cannot be understated. It is the conduit for connection and relationship building, the thread which weaves families into a unified tapestry. Playfulness also builds warmth and connection within the church family. Some congregations forget to play together. Yet it serves as a significant part of building an antidote to the fallout of trauma. Joy plants the seeds of hope and increases the desire to spend time together. We want to share experiences with people who help us feel happy. Playfulness and good humor build deposits in the family's Emotional Bank Accounts and provide an important buffer for the inevitable withdrawals of stress, trauma, and general life challenges. It is the ribbon that ties the gift of belonging.

Steven Covey developed the Emotional Bank Account[65] concept to describe the fluctuating ebb and flow of trust and connection in relationships.[66] When "withdrawals" exceed "deposits" the relationship is in danger of fracture. Making playfulness and fun a priority helps ensure that the balance in a relationship always tips toward the positive. The concept of an Emotional Bank Account serves as an apt descriptor for all relationships—family, social, and spiritual.

Faith communities want to build a sense of belonging and connection, of meeting and understanding the needs of

---

[65] http://www.evokepotential.com/284/

[66] Covey Stephen. *The Seven Habits of Highly Effective People.* Cambridge: Simon & Schuster; 1989

adoptees and their families. Like the parent-child relationship, the faith community can strengthen their connection with congregants by balancing experiences of support, healing, and joy with those that emphasize discipleship, service, and repentance. Ensure that the relationship does not tip toward the negativity of judgment and criticism. Sponsor activities for families to engage with their faith communities in ways filled with joy and fun.

Integrate Child's Birth Heritage

It is primarily the responsibility of the adoptive family to nurture respect for and connection to a child's birth heritage. But faith communities have a role to play here as well; they can support and encourage the adoptee's need to know and have her or his heritage valued. Many adult adoptees reported that they were told by church members that it was sinful for them to be curious about their genealogical roots. Their curiosity was perceived as second-guessing God.

As previously mentioned, current neurobiological and psychiatric research has demonstrated the fundamental urge that *all* persons need to know who they are and from whence they arose. Adoption does not erase the hunger for information or the benefits of such knowledge. Adoptees have an even deeper primal need for this information because they must braid the two strands of adoptive and biological history into a healthy and cohesive identity. This is a daunting task that is emotionally, intellectually, and spiritually challenging. Adoptees need support from their faith communities.

Honor Child's Need to Know and Connect with Birth Family

Parents can and do love all their children. No one questions that fact. Equally true, a child can love more than one family. Adoptees are capable of loving all of their relatives—birth and adoptive. Love is not a zero-sum game. Every loving relationship enriches. It is unfair and unreasonable to expect an adoptee to choose between his birth family and his adoptive family. They need both. To insist that they deny or ignore their desire to know and/or interact with their birth families is unfair and unhealthy. Moreover, it contradicts the research and best practices currently advocated.[67]

As parents have come to understand their children's adoption-connected needs better, they realize that they do not need to feel threatened by the vital and permanent role which birth families have for their children. Although the dynamics differ with every family, adoption joins birth and adoptive families through their mutual commitment to the well-being of their children. This openness is not co-parenting, but co-loving.

Faith communities can honor this essential bond by respecting it and by not advocating for undivided loyalty to

---

[67] NACAC (North American Council on Adoptable Children) https://www.nacac.org/advocate/nacacs-positions/#records, Donaldson Adoption Institute https://www.adoptioninstitute.org/policy-advocacy/

the adoptive family. Expecting adoptees to choose one or the other requires adoptees to sacrifice part of themselves. It is like asking them to choose to breathe or to eat. Both functions are essential to sustain life. Jesus expanded his circle of followers and called them brothers and sisters. His love did not decrease, but increased. Similarly, adoptees can make space for both their birth and adoptive inheritances.

> *"Faith teaches us to be honest. This should carry over to the way we approach adoptees. It's our right to know who we are."* –Lynn. M.

Gather Special Mementos (Especially in Closed Adoptions)

Adoptive parents—and/or anyone facilitating the placement—should preserve information and gather items before the opportunity is lost. Gather photos, video or audio messages, and special trinkets. These items become treasured heirlooms after adoption, ones that connect an adoptee to her family of origin. Write down whatever is known about family histories. (Include all information, even the difficult or painful, but ensure that information is shared at age appropriate times and presented with compassion.) Create maps that reflect their geographic origins. Compile profiles of family occupations. Every piece of data has value! Even the tiniest bit can help adoptees cope. Keep these items in a secure place. Preserve the originals and share copies with young adoptees.

Nurture Child's Innate Talents

In their eagerness to "claim" their children, adoptive parents often focus on identifying and nurturing the ways in which their children reflect similarities with the adoptive family. This strengthens their sense of connection. It is vital, however, that families and communities express an equal appreciation and encouragement of the ways adoptees differ from their adoptive families. This balance of valuation and encouragement benefits both parents and children. Their differences contribute a fresh "ingredient" to traditional family patterns. Respecting and nurturing their differences allows adoptees the freedom to pursue their innate talents and inclinations. This freedom is essential to their mental health.

Faith communities can join parents in nurturing a child's gifts. The Bible admonishes us not to keep our "light under a bushel."[68] Similarly it highlights how each of us possesses different talents for which we will be held accountable. Since we have gifts that differ according to the grace given to us, each of us is expected to exercise them accordingly.[69] Our aptitudes are God's gift to us. What we do with them is our gift to God. We must not impede adoptees' ability to reciprocate God's blessing to them.

---

[68] Matthew 5:14-16

[69] Romans 12:6

Parents Must Resolve Their Own Grief and Loss Issues

Most of this chapter has focused on how families and congregations can support and encourage adoptees and first families. It is also essential, however, that adoptive parents look inward to identify and acknowledge their own individual needs, challenges, and "baggage." This is especially critical for those who turned to adoption after infertility. Adoption enables infertile individuals and couples to become parents; it does not cure infertility. The shift from the pursuit of pregnancy to the choice to adopt requires a significant realignment of expectations and dreams.

Infertility cuts a permanent and deep-seated loss which will influence thoughts, feelings, and beliefs across lifetimes. Often this happens on an unconscious level. Even in families where infertility was/is not a factor, the loss of genetic connection is real and permanent. Parents must do the inner work of examining and resolving any issues which result. This is not a one-and-done analysis; it is a factor which needs periodic revisiting. If not handled, these feelings can adversely affect attachment patterns and mental health of all members of the family.

When counseling adoptive parents, faith communities can assist them in confronting these complicated emotions. Blend compassion with neutrality and help them resolve these sensitive issues. Adoption is utterly steeped in both/and dualities, and faith communities can bear witness, offer comfort, and channel the healing of God's love.

Questions to Consider

1. As a parent, how does Adoption-attunement redefine your understanding of the benefits of adoption as well as the coexistence of loss and gain after adoption?

2. What are the benefits of parents addressing their own grief and loss issues?

3. How does the recognition that adoption reshapes every family member deepen your appreciation for the challenges that adoptive families face?

Steps to Take

1. Follow the Golden Rule when counseling expectant mothers and adoptees.

2. Become clear on the genuine losses which adoption creates.

3. Help create the open, receptive forum adoptees seek on both a personal, family and congregational level.

CHAPTER 8

Rethink God's Will as a Justification for Adoption

"I'm certain God did not intend to break up a family to provide someone else with a child." —*Anonymous*

One action families and faith can take to embrace adoptees is to refrain from declaring that adoption was God's will. Of all pronouncements commonly made about adoption, this explanation is guaranteed to alienate an adoptee. Many respondents emphasized this sentiment.

Before Sally and Dan received their first child through adoption, they shared many conversations about why they wanted to adopt. Since Sally had experienced adoption in her family of origin, adoption was a possibility for her in

CHAPTER 8:
RETHINK GOD'S WILL AS A JUSTIFICATION FOR ADOPTION

forming a family. Dan was in full agreement because they both desired to help and love a child in need. They felt called by God to be adoptive parents.

The adoption of their first child was exciting. They were overjoyed when they received a son to love and parent. And they were helping an orphan at the same time. They had little knowledge of the circumstances of their son's first family, but they had enough information for them to know that he needed a home and a family. The joy, the satisfying feeling of helping a child in need, the assurance that they were doing the right thing for this orphaned child—all these validated their decision to adopt.

However, with their second adoption, validating the adoption became more complex. Instead of minimal background information they actually met their daughter's first mother while she was pregnant. They learned her personal story and saw firsthand the pain in her decision to place her child for adoption. Life circumstances—not personal desire or God's call—tore her baby away from her.

Their third child's experience pressed them to question the statement, "It was God's will."

Their third child was a soon-to-be teenager at the time of her adoption. They were introduced to the years of foster care and the struggles of her first family. Never before had they been so close to the complexities and almost-impossible situations that poverty and oppression cause.
Sally and Dan no longer could give an over-arching reason for adoption that made the process free from complexity. They realized that they actually had no business attempting

an answer as to the "why" of adoption. No easy answer applied. When any child is adopted from foster care, a dream of a reunified family no longer remains a possibility. That is a heavy burden for a child. Yes, their daughter needed a family and they were glad to be that family. Their joy was no longer unbounded. It was tempered with a deep empathy for her heartache. Justifying why they were brought together became far more complex and truly beyond their ability to resolve completely.

Adoptive parents face the task of explaining why they are adopting a child. Even before the adoption process begins, they ask themselves, *Why do we want to adopt?* Then, they need to sit before social workers and others who ask them the same question. Finally, the question comes again and again from family, friends, and curious strangers.

The question reveals that the adoption of a child requires that people must have good reasons for wanting to parent a child. They can feel the pressure to give persuasive explanations that justify adoption and them as an adoptive family.

When Sally and Dan tried to answer the "why" of adoption, they were uneasy with their responses because, deep down, they knew that no simple answer exists. There is something inherently painful in adoption, something that parents, professionals, and society try to explain and normalize.

The temptation is to relieve the pain and controversy by declaring that God willed the adoption experience. We hear

CHAPTER 8:
RETHINK GOD'S WILL AS A JUSTIFICATION FOR ADOPTION

these words spoken to adoptees from adoptive parent's lips, from social workers, from church members, from clergy:

It was God's will.
God meant you to be with us from the beginning.
This was God's plan for you.

After their personal adoption experiences Sally and Dan began to see that they could not answer why their children were placed for adoption and why they were not with their first families. They could give the known circumstances of their adoptions, but that was not the same as having the answer to "why."

Only first families and adoptees can make sense of their individual adoption experiences. Adoptive parents and congregations stand outside the initial loss and disruption. Others were not there when the first mothers or first families began the journey that brought children to us. No one can know the depth of the struggle or the complexities of the situation to be able to say, "This was meant to be," or "It was God's will." In fact, as difficult as it is to consider, some may not know for certain that the children's separation from their birth families was voluntary.

The complex nature of how children come to be adopted calls into question the use of God's will as a reason for adoption. In this chapter we re-examine how the faithful in the Bible understand God's will and God's activity in their struggles and use our new awareness to help us with the question of "Why?"

The Use of God's Will in the Bible

We can see throughout the Bible that God's people have struggled to discern God's will. Often, we see that the question of God's plan bubbles up when tragedy strikes. Did God want this or cause this? God's faithful looked for divine will in the Babylonian Exile, in the wilderness, in the persecutions, and in the imprisonments.

Prophets arose to help God's people interpret what was happening to them, how God was involved, and what God's desire was for them. Moses was one such prophet who named some of the Israelite's behaviors as unfaithfulness and interpreted some of the suffering as consequences. (See the Hebrew Scriptures of Genesis through Joshua.)

It is important to note that the discernment of God's will most often takes place between God and the people who were experiencing the loss. Bound together by difficulty God's people listened for God's voice and looked for God's activity. Collectively, they made inferences on what pain came from the hand of God and what came from the hands of humans.

One potential exception is the story of Job and his well-meaning friends. Throughout the entire book Job struggles to find the answer for his suffering while his friends continue to assert that it is, in some way, Job's fault that he lost his family and all that he had. However, the book of Job actually reinforces the assertion that only those experiencing loss can seek its meaning for in the end, the friends are of no real help. Instead, it is the private conversation between God and Job which brings resolution and renewal.

CHAPTER 8:
RETHINK GOD'S WILL AS A JUSTIFICATION FOR ADOPTION

We also might be inclined to lift up the story of Joseph as a testimony to the possibility of separation being God's will. We know the story well: Joseph's brothers are jealous of him. They plot to sell him as a slave and lead their father to believe that Joseph is killed by an animal. Joseph winds up in the hands of the Egyptians and their father is in the throes of lifelong grief.

As the story goes the Egyptians discover Joseph's talent to foresee the future in his own dreams and to interpret the dreams of others, including the dreams of the king of Egypt himself. Joseph rises through the ranks and eventually sits alongside the king as his governor. Due to a famine in his homeland Joseph's brothers make their way to Egypt to beg for food at the feet of their brother whom they do not recognize.[70]

Joseph takes this opportunity to reveal himself to them and offer mercy. He says, "Don't be afraid. Do I act for God? Don't you see, you planned evil against me but God used those same plans for my good, as you see all around you right now—life for many people."[71] We as adoptive parents and faith communities may look at this story as an example of God's will. We could say that sometimes God intends the rupture of first families for the sake of a greater good. We could conclude that God intended this life for Joseph in order that many would be saved.

---

[70] Genesis 37 and following

[71] Genesis 50:19-20, The Message, Eugene Peterson

However, does that line of thinking hold up and ring true?

As we look closely at this text, we first can see that Joseph, although he struggles with what to do, does not appear to be in the throes of distress or danger when he addresses his brothers and speaks of God's intention. Now an adult, he reflects on his trauma as a youth, and speaks from a place of power. Just as he could see into the future through interpretation of dreams, Joseph sees into the past and interprets the meaning of his fractured life.

Second, we notice that it is Joseph who interprets and speaks of God's involvement in what happened to him. We do not hear the brothers justify the pain they caused by claiming that God used it for the greater good. We do not read that the King of Egypt or any other Egyptians whom Joseph encountered along the way make such a claim for why Joseph was torn from his people. Only the one who endured, only Joseph, is the one who can offer an interpretation that it is God's hand that reshapes his tragedy.

Joseph makes a remarkable claim about God's ability to reach into his life, however painful, and direct it toward something good. God made Joseph's separation and struggle count for something. It is vital to emphasize that Joseph does not dismiss the evil intentions of his brothers when he elevates God's ability. Instead, Joseph acknowledges his brothers' evil intentions and by doing so validates his own painful experience. He does not identify his family's betrayal as divinely ordained. He does affirm God's ability to respond and direct such evil toward good.

CHAPTER 8:
RETHINK GOD'S WILL AS A JUSTIFICATION FOR ADOPTION

The discussion of God's will in orchestrating the separation of a family only can occur between God and those who experienced the initial pain and loss that led to adoption: first families and especially the children who are no longer with them. Human decisions can cause extremely challenging circumstances and people, not God, decide adoption is the appropriate solution.

A survey respondent reflects:

> *My own adoption story is NOT a story of sacrificial love so great that I was given a chance at a "better life." My own personal adoption story involves a man who did not want to be a father, and so he manipulated, extorted, and abused his wife into placing all of their children for adoption with other families."* —Rebekah H

Just as Sally and Dan inserted themselves into an experience that was not theirs when they said, *It was meant to be*, The Church often has done the same. Like Job's friends, we as The Church have offered to adoptees and first mothers or families reasons why we think the separation occurred. From the pulpit we have declared that adoption is God's will and promoted it in the context of encouraging families to adopt. *It was God's will for you* has been offered to adoptees and first mothers as an effort to either comfort them or assure them that their loss has meaning and purpose. By extension, the belief that adoption is God's will is often used to reassure, soothe, and legitimize adoptive parents in their new role. However, adoptees find this "ordained by God" idea hurtful and dismissive.

Sally finds it helpful to think of how she and her husband coped with infertility. Their struggle and their loss were personal, something that their family unit of two experienced. Although family, friends, and faith community could be supportive, it was between God, Sally, and Dan to understand God's hand in lives. Had some counseled them and said, "It is God's will" or "This was meant to be," Sally and Dan would have questioned that person's motive and their lack of understanding since they stood outside of Sally and Dan's experience. Much damage is done to our children when we impose God's will on the painful experience of the loss of their first family. Throughout the respondents' comments we noticed that the greatest damage of all was a turning away from God, an abandonment of faith.

We hear an adoptee's despair and alienation:

> *"Since my adoption was God's will, I hated God."*
>
> *—Sharon W.*

Another adoptee shares powerful feelings about her view of God's role.

> *"Those who benefit by taking the children of other parents claim this is "God's plan." They have created a monstrous "God" who uses the bodies of the vulnerable to favor the privileged. This is not the loving God of the Bible."*
>
> *—Sarah M.*

CHAPTER 8:
RETHINK GOD'S WILL AS A JUSTIFICATION FOR ADOPTION

As we read the insights above, both Sally and Gayle could relate to the parent-centric and faith-validating point of view to which these adoptees responded. They were there, as parents, silently longing for a connection so deep as if they had birthed their children, wanting that primal tie. Sally was there, as a pastor, believing that from the beginning of her children's lives, God planned for her to be their parent.

For their own need to validate adoption Sally and Gayle eclipsed their children's experiences and ignored God's creative work. They distorted God's original intention for our children for own benefit and peace of mind.

Psalm 139 clearly states God's intention and God's creative power. The Psalmist says, "For it was you who formed my inward parts; you knit me together in my mother's womb. I praise you, for I am fearfully and wonderfully made."[72] God created mother and child to be beautiful and complete. There is a movement in this Psalm of connection and celebration between the first mother and her child.

When adoptees hear that it is God's will that they are not with their first mother or family, the idea is incompatible with the connecting-loving-creating God they read about in Scripture. Instead, our well-meaning interpretation of their life events introduces them to a disruptive-destructive-dismissive God. For many adoptees we create confu-

---

[72] Psalm 139:13-14, NRSV

sion rather than comfort and promote pain rather than promise.

Which God is it that our children encounter in our homes and congregations? A God who destroys God's very good creation or a God who loves creation? When our beliefs identify family separation as divinely ordained this predisposes us to ignore, overlook, underestimate, and/or justify the painful legacy of adoption. It also gives us permission to accept the external factors that lead to adoption, like poverty, lack of resources, and social injustice.

What Can We Say about God's Role in Adoption?

> *"I truly believe it was not HIS plan, but my birth mother's shame that prompted my adoption. Was God there for me and did he protect and guide me and make sure I was ok? Yes, He did. But there is a big leap from that line of thinking to GOD WANTED YOU ADOPTED. I just don't believe that God sends down biological children and decides "yep, that one is going to be adopted." Of course, he KNOWS, but it is the free will of our birth mothers that causes us to be relinquished." —Lynn G.*

> *"When I was very young, I realized that Jesus's mother was unmarried when she got pregnant, just like my mother. I wasn't very happy that God thought it was okay to save some mothers from a bad situation but not other mothers." —Jean S.*

CHAPTER 8:
RETHINK GOD'S WILL AS A JUSTIFICATION FOR ADOPTION•

If we as adoptive parents and congregations are not in a position to say that the adoption was God's will, then what, if anything, can we say about God's role?

First, we can say that God grieves with adoptees and first families. God is present in their pain and does not desire such a primal loss just as God does not desire any kind of illness or loss for any of us. We know that Scripture reveals this grieving God and shows us how God desires to comfort those who suffer.[73]

Second, we can say that God works to prevent suffering and calls us to eliminate the root circumstances that lead to the rupture of families. Instead of promoting adoption as a God-driven event, we now see advocacy for eliminating injustice, oppression, hunger, and other societal inequalities as our primary call. Adoption, then, may become a vehicle of God's healing, although not all adoption experiences bear this out.

Scripture also reveals to us the length to which God will go to preserve first families and communities. We see this throughout the Hebrew Bible where God desires the Israelites to be freed from slavery, saved, and sent to a land where they can flourish as a people. We see this in the New Testament where God sends Christ to reunite and restore God's relationship with us. In the ultimate act of commitment God offered the sacrifice of His Son to restore the relationship and bring us back home.

---

[73] Jeremiah 29:11; Psalm 22:24; Psalm 100:5; John 3:16; II Cor. 1:4, NRSV

The Church as a Space for Questions about God's Will in Adoption

> *"The church needs to be a place ... that helps [adoptees] put the pieces of the puzzle together."* —Carla B.

Just like adoptive families want their homes to be safe places and embody God's love, adoptees need their faith communities to be places of safety and reflections of God's welcoming love. The Church already is poised to offer this kind of space and acceptance in liturgy, sermons, prayers and its fellowship. Adoptees will experience the validation they are seeking when The Church's worship life and fellowship are steeped in empathy and understanding for adoptees. Just as importantly adoptive children will hear in the teaching, the preaching, the praying, and the communing, that painful separation is never desired or driven by God.

"Lolita", a fosteree/adoptee, offers a powerful view:

> *"If you put God [in adoption] it becomes, 'God help us both. God, help me lead and guide this child in the way you want.' It's not your idea [of what guidance is best] for this child, it's God's idea. It could be different from what you want, like your values, your beliefs...you need to align your plan with what God would have you do for this child. This goes for the church family, as well."* —Lolita

God's role in adoption is to grieve with children and families and to bring healing and hope through our advoca-

CHAPTER 8:
RETHINK GOD'S WILL AS A JUSTIFICATION FOR ADOPTION

cy and our listening. As adoptive families and faith communities we may be able to help adoptees draw the distinction between God's will and God's ability to create goodness out of pain. We stand in solidarity with adoptees as we look at God and God's Word from their point of view.

An adoptive parent realizes,

> *"Adoption is not something we can figure out or fix by declaring it is God's will'."* —Anonymous

Instead, we hold a place for the painful separation experience of which we were not a part. We stand aside to let adoptees and first families wrestle with God's presence in their loss and trust them to discern and find meaning in their experiences. We invite them to consider that God grieves with them. We step in—carefully, respectfully —as participants in God's ability to create something beautiful— such as an adoptive family— out of pain.

Many of us who are parents will be the first responders to our children's question, "Why?" Occasionally church leaders or members may be asked this question by an adoptee who is seeking to make sense of his or her life.

When we attempt to respond and comfort, we offer these suggestions. We do not need to have an explanation or all the answers. As hard as it is to see our children struggle, we can walk alongside them in their questioning and wonder aloud with them. We can explore with them which answers, if any, they are considering. We can validate their pain and honor it by not dismissing it.

We can affirm carefully, humbly, and gently our position through our own experience of loss in life and the experience we find in the Bible that God does not desire children to be separated from their first families, but people can heal and thrive. We can, if the time seems right, express what we have learned from our own experience, that even in the midst of pain and even out of suffering, God can create something good and beautiful.[74] One such good and beautiful thing might be our family.

While it is certainly possible for God to bring forth a solution, the fracturing of a family to heal the barrenness of another is troubling at best. God is not in the business of destroying lives but of healing them.

Questions to Consider:

1. How has your family and your congregation explained the reasons for adoption?

2. What new perspective have you learned regarding divine will and adoption?

3. How can you create more space for your child to make sense of his/her own adoption experience and encourage your congregation to do the same?

Steps to Take

---

[74] Romans 8: 28-29, NRSV

CHAPTER 8:
Rethink God's Will as a Justification for Adoption

1. Demonstrate through preaching, teaching, liturgy, and prayers that God does not desire painful experiences such as family separation.

2. Be open to hearing the concerns of adoptees without trying to *solve* their concerns or explaining their situation as "God's will."

3. Minister to the widow and the orphan, preferably as an intact unit.

CHAPTER 9

The Power of Words: Language Matters

> "In the beginning was the Word, and the Word was with God, and the Word was God."
> —John 1:1

Use Sound Adoption Language

The Bible affirms the positive power of words. It identifies Jesus as the Word made flesh. In the most generative aspect words can reflect the divine power of creation. They can also isolate or include, judge or accept, inspire or defeat, heal or hurt, soothe or insult, unify or divide.

Language shapes our experience. Words carry meaning beyond their literal definition. Consider these pairs: slender/skeletal or unique/weird. Feel the distinct emotional weight between them. The first word in each pair feels neutral while the second one carries an implied negative judgment. Emotion-charged words have a place, but sometimes we *want* to use language that softens. At other times we need language that evokes raw emotion. Both serve important communication purposes. The key thing is to use language intentionally.

When discussing adoption —a situation steeped in profound and often conflicting emotions —words make a huge difference. We strive to package, describe, or bound those feelings. Literal language often falls short so we turn to metaphor.

Adoption is often described as grafting a child to a new family tree. The comparison is understandable, yet incomplete. It is vital that we do not lose sight of the fact that it is a person who is being adopted. Many people think of these children as "blank slates" who, once placed in their new families, will carry no memories, need no connection and reflect no influence from their first families. Adoption-attunement affirms that children are neither blank slates nor are they clay waiting for adoptive families to shape into their own image. They are human beings with unique predispositions and potential that will be formed and defined by both nature and nurture. These influences do not neutralize one another; they co-exist, ebb and flow, and persist throughout the adoptee's lifetime.

Unwanted. Abandoned. Given away. Imagine a child hearing these or other similar words which adoptees hear throughout their lives. Even if the intent was not to offend, the words still sting. Once heard, these phrases and ideas cannot be "unheard." They lodge in memory and reinforce feelings of rejection, abandonment, and inadequacy. Such words cut deeply into an adoptee's already-fragile self-esteem.

The concept of Positive Adoption Language took hold to counter these negative results. PAL must be used with awareness because it can be a two-edged sword. PAL strives to couch some of the "hard stuff" with more empathy, sensitivity, and consideration for complexity. For example, *made an adoption* plan replaced *gave up* or *gave away*. But sometimes it can be used to candy-coat and minimize adoption loss.

PAL gained traction among professionals and adoptive families; however, many people remain uninformed. By default, they rely on the less sensitive language of the past. This often includes faith communities at both the pastoral and lay levels. Until educated on the topic, old patterns prevail. Remember, *all* of the relationships involved in an adoption are real; the word does not pertain only to genetic relationships.

Positive Adoption Language	**Language to Avoid**
Birth child	Real child
Birth Parent or First Parent	Real parent
Planned an adoption	Gave away, Relinquished,

	Gave up, Didn't want
Chose to parent	Kept her child
Was adopted	Is adopted
Traditional	Closed Adoption
Terminated parental rights	Taken away
In need of a family	Unwanted
Birth family, first family	Real Family
Born to unmarried parents	Illegitimate
International adoption	Foreign adoption

"Unsanitized" Language Serves an Important Purpose Too

Sound or Positive Adoption Language (PAL) has a valued role in adoption-related conversations, but adoption therapist and adult adoptee L. J. asks faith communities to address the adoption experience "With truth, transparency and 'real' language." Adult adoptees tell us that they also want—need—some conversations to use "unsanitized"

Lnguage that does not take the sting out of the circumstance being described.

Most adoptees do, in fact, feel given away, rejected, unwanted. All the logic in the world does not change their emotions. They want faith communities to feel the weight of these heavy emotions and to bear witness to their personal Gethsemane experiences. Faith communities have an opportunity to channel the comfort and healing of God when they welcome the light of truth and toss aside platitudes or simplistic bromides. From this stance of honesty, they help adoptees carry the weight of their personal crosses.

Language Has Sometimes Been Used as a Tool to Drive a Specific Outcome.

Language can be crafted to remove the sting of truth, to obscure the emotional and psychic costs of adoption, and to convince an expectant mother and father that adoption is an entirely rosy option. This is manipulative, misleading, and unethical.

Expectant parents deserve the courtesy of the unvarnished truth with all its emotional resonance intact. This truth-telling allows them to make an informed, fact-based decision either to parent or make an adoption plan for their child. After all, there is no backtracking from an adoption. It permanently divides the lives of all involved into a *Before and After* reality from which there is no escape. Birth parents must receive the full truth of what adoption will mean for them and their children. (Keep in mind that a child's adoption also affects any other siblings or subsequent children whom her mother and/or father chooses to parent as well as future generations.) Moreover, conversations should first focus on keeping mothers and/or fathers and their children together.

We must imagine ourselves in this mother's shoes, and then follow the Golden Rule as we strive to guide and support her. To do any less is to betray her trust at a vulnerable time when she is relying on The Church for assistance. Avoid identifying improved financial circumstances as adequate justification for a child's adoption. Poverty is an insufficient reason for separating a child from his or her family. Ensure that the language used is non-coercive and in the best interest of mother and child.

Choose language with intention, compassion, and integrity. Understand why specific words and phrases can offend, manipulate, or invalidate. Recognize when it is appropriate and important to use language from which the emotion has *not* been sanitized.

To increase a sense of belonging, our language attunement regarding adoption must extend to the pulpit, the Sunday school classroom, and beyond. An awareness of the tone and emotional weight of words is essential. We must also set a conscious intention for our actions and conversations. Get clear on the purpose of a conversation before saying anything.

Parents, professionals, and faith communities share a common desire: to be a source of comfort, support, and understanding for adoptees, first and adoptive families. Every adoption-connected conversation must further these positive intentions.

Speak with Clarity

Faith communities can best serve adoptees by ensuring that adoption-related conversations are steeped in truth and accuracy, free of cultural bias and assumptions. Hold conversations that mention not only the benefits but also the heartbreaking aspects of adoption. God's role is not diminished when we make space for human complexity. This means conversations must acknowledge that adoption begins with the primal, deep, and pervasive injury of separation from mother and first family. Validate and empathize. Avoid platitudes. Be with them instead of talking at them. Bear witness and help them shoulder their cross.

Recall David Augsberger's words mentioned earlier: "Being heard is so close to being loved, that for the average person, the two are almost indistinguishable."[75] This deep level of listening validates and provides compassionate witness and becomes Christian love in action.

Listen instead of lecture. Learn what adoptees want and need. Listen to each story individually. Each situation is unique. Do not presume to know God's will or what has been divinely ordained. Listening is a gift. Listening with an open heart and mind is a rare blessing.

When asked how faith communities might better address the adoptee experience one respondent answered,

> *"My first thought is that the population is so low that the rest of the congregation might feel a bit highjacked. In a church community of 200, would there be even five or ten adoptees?"* —Rayne W.

Her remark—that adoptees are a minor part of faith community membership—reflects the isolation adoptees

---

[75] Augsberger, David. Quoted by Leslie Booker. SoundsTrue.com. Embodying Radical Presence: Awareness of Race, Culture, and Self in Healing Trauma.

and first mothers often feel. This results in large part from people's tendency to "hide" their adoption connection. Guilt, shame, and a deep desire for privacy all contribute to this need to cover up adoption. This builds a misperception that adoption touches a very narrow group—only adoptees themselves.

In fact, adoption touches many lives, not only adopted children, their siblings and their adoptive parents, but also birth parents, extended families, life partners, children and grandchildren of adoptees, etc. According to a 1997 report compiled by the Evan B. Donaldson Adoption Institute, "58 percent of Americans know someone who has been adopted, has adopted a child or has relinquished a child for adoption."[76] U.S. government statistics report that 53,549 children are adopted from foster care.[77] An unreported number were adopted privately or through non-governmental agencies as well as via international adoptions. This represents a lot of people. Faith communities can recognize that by embracing Adoption-attunement, they will benefit a large swath of their followers and will provide the best support they can offer.

The cultural pressure adoptees experience to keep the range of their feelings under wraps has a profound influence on the way adoptees perceive and experience relationship. The link between love and relinquishment, the expectation to prettify and deny their loss, the fear that abandon-

---

[76] http://www.pbs.org/pov/offandrunning/fact-sheet/

[77] https://www.acf.hhs.gov/sites/default/files/cb/afcarsreport23.pdf

ment can reoccur if one's authentic self is revealed, the obligation to pretend their lives are different than they actually are—all these forces add up to challenge their ability to trust, to express their truth, and to know that they are good enough.

Faith communities can be part of an updated, educated support system that helps adoptees overcome this baggage. Positive intention is a powerful and important subconscious force; however, good intentions alone, as we've mentioned earlier, are not enough. They must be accompanied by awareness, sensitivity, prudence, truth-telling, and courtesy.

Language Shapes Our Experience.

"Language," German philosopher Martin Heidegger famously said, "is the house of being."[78] It is the channel through which humans connect. The absence of language also profoundly shapes the human ability to communicate and even the ability to think.[79] This fact directly influences adoptees who were adopted before they had acquired language. Their loss-experience is encoded somatically, locked in a world where words were not yet available to bound, describe, process, and heal it. Their experiences are imprinted within their flesh.[80]

---

[78] Martin Heidegger, Letter on Humanism, https://en.wikipedia.org/wiki/Martin_Heidegger

[79] https://www.wnyc.org/radio/#/ondemand/91725

[80] Bessel van der Kolk, The Body Keeps the Score

Imagine a child hearing she was given away or that her birth parents didn't want her, that she is not her parents' own child, or other similar unsettling and painful things which adoptees hear throughout their lives.

> "When you are adopted, you hear that your new parents could not have children of their own' Whose child then, are you?" —Anne H.

Readers might gloss over this quote. That would be a mistake because it provides a poignant peek inside the mind of a young adoptee as she struggles to understand her place and permanency in her family. She hears that her parents can't have children "of their own." *Isn't she her parents' "own" child?* She calls them Mom and Dad and they call her their daughter.

Furthermore, a child does not understand that the phrase, "not able to have children of their own" refers to infertility as the cause of her parents' childlessness. A child will understand this inability through her personal experience. For her, "not able" equals "forbidden" as in "You are not able to have candy." The child may assume that her parents are forbidden (not able) to have children just as she is forbidden to have candy. The child then may then logically wonder: *How are they able to have me if they can't have children?*

Questions swirl in her head. *Aren't we a family? If I am not their own, how long will I stay in this family?* These worries leave her feeling unsettled, insecure, and frightened.

Anxiety builds within her. *Will she be removed? Where will she go? And with whom?* The most important part of her life—her family—feels endangered and impermanent. This conundrum would perplex adults; it definitely unsettles adopted children. It is easy to see how such language contributes to adoptees' fears and insecurities.

Even if unintended, these potent words still sting, still awaken uncertainty and fear, and still stir painful emotions. Once heard, these toxic phrases and ideas cannot be unheard. They lodge in memory and reinforce feelings of rejection, abandonment, and inadequacy. Such words cut deeply into an adoptee's self-esteem.

In summary, the entire adoption constellation benefits when we use language with intention and compassion; when we understand why specific words and phrases can offend or invalidate, when we distinguish between Positive Adoption Language from "unsanitized" language (language from which the emotion has not been whitewashed), and when we identify the appropriate context for each language framework.

Word Choice Must Reflect Forethought and Respect

Birth mothers receive little compassion or support. Cultural and family pressure, shame, personal embarrassment, a desire to remain masked, and an inclination to keep their pain boxed up all contribute to their isolation. Birth mothers hold an awkward place in the world's view of adoption. They are told that placing their child for adoption is the most loving, bravest, and best choice they can make. Yet birth mothers also face the world's judgment: How could you abandon your child? Her "brave" decision to "give away" her child both astonishes and appalls people.

At some level a birth mother is the absolute antithesis of the iconic mother whom our culture and our faith hold in such high regard. A mother's love is supposed to be like no other love— boundless, fierce, and courageous—but a birth mother "chooses" to abandon her child. In the ultimate mixed message both she and her child are told that this decision is an act of love. What words fit? No simple answer exists. Compassion must infuse our language.

BM, a widely used acronym for bowel movement, is often used as an abbreviation for birth mother. This shorthand demonstrates insensitivity toward the birth mother. It requires only a few more letters to type out the entire word. This choice is an easy yet powerful way of showing compassion and respect to birth mothers. Both matter.

In a further extension of respect as expressed through language, many people consider the term first mother more suitable. First mother reflects reality; she will always be her child's first mother. Birth mother, on the other hand, tends to emphasize her *functionality* rather than her *being* as a person. Other names include natural mother and biological mother; no clear "winner" rises to the top. Persuasive arguments can be made for each.

Advocates and critics have strong feelings about the common practice of prospective adoptive parents reaching out to expectant mothers facing crisis pregnancy. (Note the distinction. Until a woman gives birth to her child, she is NOT a birth mother; she is an expectant mother making decisions about her baby. Again, language counts! Calling her a birth mother before her child is born places coercive pressure and confirms a reality that is not yet decided.)

Proponents of pre-birth matching say that it delivers essential resources to the mother while she is pregnant, improves maternal and infant health, provides emotional support, and lays the foundation for a strong open adoption relationship. Safe housing, healthy food, and quality medical care benefit mother and child, all of which are good; however, providing financial support creates emotional and monetary entanglement as well. When it is the prospective adoptive parents who pay for these services, serious ethical concerns arise because it can pressure a woman to go through with an adoption plan that she no longer wants to activate simply because she cannot repay the money. She may also feel conflicted out of a sense of loyalty or gratitude to the prospective adoptive parents who have been solicitous of her during a very difficult and emotional time.

Some expectant mothers report that because of the pre-birth relationship bond built between them and the prospective adoptive parents they no longer felt entitled to keep their babies. Having engaged for many months in a joint scenario predicated on the assumption held by all parties that she will surrender her baby, there is tremendous pressure to follow through with this expectation. In reality, no one knows how she will decide until after the baby is born —particularly the expectant mother. It demands great psychic and emotional energy to end this joint-scenario mindset to choose a different ending, one in which mother and child stay together.

Mothers who reported they had second thoughts said they could not break the prospective adoptive parents' hearts so they broke their own and went through with adoptions they no longer wanted. Clearly pre-birth matching can leave already-vulnerable women more vulnerable.

Pre-birth matching also leaves the prospective adoptive parents emotionally vulnerable as they yearn to fill their deepest heart's desire for a baby. Remaining neutral in their dealing with the expectant mother is difficult, possibly even impossible. If the expectant mother changes her mind, the couple will be emotionally devastated—sometimes financially as well. Money serves as a complicating factor in many of the decisions regarding when and if an adoption occurs.

The appropriateness of pre-birth matching must be scrutinized carefully on a case-by-case basis with a clear intention not to place undue pressure on the expectant mother. An understanding must be in place that guarantees the expectant mother's freedom to rescind her intention to relinquish her child. While this keeps financial risk on the prospective parents, it is ethically necessary.

Real is Far More Than a Word

Adoptees and their families often field the question, "Who is your real ____?" (Fill in the blank with mother, father, sibling, etc.) The word real elicits a visceral response within members of the adoption constellation. Several factors cause this; for example, the subtle insinuation that either the adoptive or birth family is inferior or less-than the other. The question implies a binary belief that only one can be real. By extension the other is rendered inauthentic. This either/or perspective is damaging to adoptees and both their birth and adoptive families.

The bonds and attachments formed within an adoptive family are often doubted. People question the depth and permanency of the connection. People frequently ask adoptive parents if they still hope to have a child of their "own." In circumstances where an adopted child has significant behavioral challenges, it is quite common for her parents to be asked if they will now give her back. This absurd question would never be posed to parents raising their troubled biological offspring.

Adoptees encounter the flip side of such questions; people want to know about their "real" family. This places children in a bind because both their families are real. Part of the problem is mainly one of language. People lack the appropriate vocabulary—birth, first, or genetic—parent or sibling. But underpinning the language void is a widely held suspicion that relationships created through adoption can never be quite as intimate, dependable, or permanent as those created through biology.

Forever Families

Adoptive families typically think of themselves as the child's "forever family" to distinguish them from the birth family. At first pass this might make sense because for an adoption to occur, the birth parents' rights must be terminated. But this is an oversimplification. In fact, both adoptive and birth families are permanently part of a child's life. This is true regardless of the degree of physical contact between the adoptee and his or her first family. At the very least, they remain an essential part of the adoptee biologically and psychically. "Forever family" when attributed exclusively to the adoptive family is incomplete and it has outlived its usefulness.

When adoption occurs, it is intended to be a permanent bond. Some adoptions do end in disruption or dissolution which is a true tragedy.[81] We believe widespread acceptance of adoption-attunement and all of its ramifications would help reduce these negative outcomes. Dissolution and disruption are distinct from the odious, unethical, and morally repugnant practice of rehoming.[82] Described by the Child Welfare League of America as "underground child custody transfers … to non-vetted strangers without public child welfare agency or court approval and oversight. Rehoming is the ultimate objectification of children. Calling this practice "rehoming" is an effort to use language to cover up malignant action.

---

[81] https://www.childwelfare.gov/pubpdfs/s_disrup.pdf

[82] https://www.cwla.org/wp-content/uploads/2015/06/Joint-Statement_Responding-to-Rehoming_June2015.pdf

Words Influence Beliefs and Shape Behavior

Faith communities can embrace the concept of both/and. Birth family and adoptive family both are significant to the adoptee, and they are all a permanent and integral part of the adoptee. Faith communities can help spread this much healthier vision of adoption-shaped relationships. This reframing from either/or to a more inclusive, more respectful both/and is an important responsibility for faith communities. Language matters. Language education and awareness begins with the church hierarchy and filters down to the pastors, lay staff, congregants, and especially to any church-affiliated professionals involved in counseling or facilitating adoptions.

This scrupulous sensitivity to language and its impact on people's experiences is a simple yet vital way of delivering Christian compassion and respect for the spiritual, physical, and mental health of those touched by adoption.

Three Trigger Words: Chosen, Grateful, and Lucky

Our exploration of Adoption-attunement makes it clear that trauma, grief, and loss underpin all adoptions, even those where children have bonded with their adoptive families and were lovingly nurtured. Whether their adoptions could be considered successful or not, the words chosen, lucky, and grateful strike most adoptees with an excruciating sense of invalidation. Listen to these heartfelt words of several adoptees.

> *"Statements like 'You were chosen' don't help the pain."* — Lorraine R.

> *"Adoption brought me great love and my greatness [sic] heartache. Adoption is on my brain 24/7. How society tells me I should feel grateful, lucky, chosen. I've spent most of my life trying to straddle the fence of being the perfect, grateful daughter and the heartbroken girl who felt unloved, unwanted and unworthy."* —Anonymous

"Your Mother Loved You So Much That She Gave You Up."

Adoptees have heard this explanation for decades. Adoption professionals, adoptive parents, clergy, and the general public all subscribed to this belief. In fact, Sally and Gayle spoke these to our own children. Now that we are aware of adoption complexity, this explanation feels unsettling. This phrase purports to comfort and reassure adoptees. Instead, children gleaned a totally different message: people who love you, really love you, will give you up. They will leave and abandon you. This platitude planted seeds of mistrust and relationship insecurity that plague many adoptees for a lifetime.

While the toxic message was unintended, it is what was learned because it was based on incontrovertible evidence: the mother who conceived, carried, and gave birth to the child gave him or her away. Out of love. That is pretty convincing proof. Sadly, another inference most adoptees draw is that the adoption is their fault, that something about them was inadequate or unacceptable and caused their adoption. That is a very destructive self-belief.

> *"For me I always thought, 'Who gives their child away? Was I damaged goods from day one and my parents knew this?'"* —
>
> *Lorraine R.*

Clearly the way we speak about adoption must be recast in healthier language. The most carefully constructed language, however, cannot remove the profound and painful reality of separation which adoption creates, nor can it change this fundamental truth: their mothers could not/did not keep their children. However valid the reasons that drove these women to choose adoption, children lost their first families. Since it happened once, it is understandable for adoptees to fear it could happen again.

Gift from God

Although Divine will was discussed in detail in Chapter Three, we still wanted to connect it to the responses adoptees wrote. Our survey reflected a nearly unanimous rejection of any suggestion that identifies adoption as a gift from God. Respondents reject the concept. They indicated that it made them feel as if their lives had been sacrificed, upended, and realigned in order to fulfill their parents' desire to adopt and/or cure their parents' infertility. They assert this belief distorts God's role in adoption. They reject a concept of a God who cures infertility by subjecting vulnerable children to the loss of their first family, culture, and country.

> *"I strongly dislike the church propagating the idea that GOD LOVES ADOPTION SO MUCH THAT HE WANTED SOME OF US TO BE RELINQUISHED. Yuck is all I can say."* —Lynn G.

When adoptive parents believe their child is a gift from God, it justifies the suffering of adoptees and their first parents to accomplish a priority of relieving infertility or fulfilling the prospective adoptive parent's yearning for a child through adoption. It seeks to justify the human cost as well as to validate the adoptive parents' claim to their child. However, we believe it is a misguided and painful strategy. As mentioned in an earlier chapter, this belief also drives a wedge between many adoptees and their faith because they resent being offered as sacrificial lambs.

Some suggest it is a way for God to bring a specific child to a specific adoptive family. If one believes that through God all things are possible, it seems unlikely that God would choose such a cruel way of bringing parent and child together.

Listen and Allow Adoptees to Relate Their Unique Personal Stories.

> *"I believe that forums that allow adoptees the opportunity to discuss their experiences without judgment would be helpful."* — Becky D.

Positive intention and awareness about our language choices brings us only so far. In order to update any preconceived and/or outdated presuppositions about adoption, we also must ensure that we listen to those who are living the reality of adoption. To ignore their voices is unkind, unchristian, and unhealthy. It also contravenes our ability to serve and support. In order to understand their experience, we must allow them the space and time to be heard without rebuttal or fear of offending us, and without our imposing a preconceived, pre-defined notion of their needs and responsibilities.

For too long, we have presumed to know what adoptees and first parents need. To truly meet another's needs we must first accurately identify them. We cannot rely on guesses, presuppositions, or what we might need in similar circumstances. Instead, ask them what they need. Then listen without refutation or blaming them for their circumstances. Fault-finding is counterproductive. Focus on identifying needs and then determine the best ways to address those needs. As we know and understand better, we can support and assist in better ways. Each person's story is unique, yet some common denominators occur in most of them. Still, no single adoptee, first family, or adoptive family experience defines the common experience of all. This is yet another reason why we must listen and not assume we know what they are feeling or that we know what they need or should be doing or feeling.

> *"A big problem in the church is that people who have no experience with adoption are talking about it like they're*

> *authorities. They're not. Only people who were actually adopted can accurately share the good and bad."*
>
> —*Rebekah H.*

> *"Freedom of healing permanently is expressed and done with Love from our faith communities. Love is done by Listening and being open to hear what each heart is feeling."*
> —*Anonymous*

It is hubris to believe that we know what is best. When it comes to adoption-related conversations listen with truth as the primary filter. While remaining committed to our Christian values, forgiveness must supersede any sense of judgment which is rightfully the purview of God. Social mores have evolved. Out-of-wedlock pregnancy is no longer viewed as an insurmountable shame for mother or child. The social stigma of unwed pregnancy or bastardy no longer exists. Every baby deserves to be welcomed, celebrated, and loved. Consider the words of Poet Laureate, Carl Sandburg who said, "A baby is God's opinion that life should go on." Regardless of the circumstances of a baby's conception, the child is not a sin.

> *"Faith teaches us to be honest. This should carry over to the way we approach adoptees."* —*Lynn M.*

Only those who have lived the experience of adoption truly understand its effects which cause trauma and lifelong fallout. We must not allow overly optimistic expectations to deafen us to their voices. We must set aside the old paradigm and with open, empathetic hearts listen to learn and to discern how we can best embody Christian love and kindness. Through our actions God's love walks the earth.

> *"Listen to the voices of ALL adoptees... Dig deeper before promoting adoption." —Anonymous*

Questions to Consider

1. How have I arrived at my beliefs about adoption, faith, and God?

2. How well do I understand the distinctions in language choices available to discuss adoption?

3. How has this discussion of language refined my attitudes and reshaped my conversations?

Steps to Take

1. Check for bias in your language when speaking about adoption.

2. Educate others when you hear insensitivity or bias in adoption conversations.

3. Resist the inclination to glorify adoption or sanitize adoption grief.

4. Discern when to use Positive Adoption Language and when to use "unsanitized" language that expresses the pain and grief that accompany adoption trauma.

Chapter 9: The Power of Words: Language Matters

CHAPTER 10

Acknowledge and Address Racism and White Privilege in The Church

Like many adoptive families, it wasn't until our children of color joined our families and we personally observed and experienced how the world treated our children and our families—it wasn't until then—that racism and prejudice became visible and real.

Even so, the discussion in this chapter may not be an easy one. It requires us to acknowledge the presence of racism and white privilege in our society as a whole. Imagine for a moment that a limited number of seats are available. One hundred people all want one. If these folks stand in a queue, someone stands in the first place; someone else stands in last. How equal are their opportunities to secure a seat? Now imagine everyone stands shoulder to shoulder. Once the advantage of being at the front of the line is gone, the inequity of privilege is removed.

We probably all say we support equality and believe that fact when we express that sentiment. But until we are willing to surrender the advantage of being at the "front of the line," the inequity of privilege will remain. It is challenging to consider surrendering a familiar system that has served us well. Reluctance is understandable; however, it is not equitable.

Supporting the *idea* of equality of access and opportunity is a start. This philosophical stance must partner with a willingness to relinquish some of the advantages which have smoothed our path so that a level playing field can emerge. Christianity requires us to think of others, to be servant leaders, and to work to ensure that everyone has access to opportunity and resources. We are called to be the Golden Rule in action.

Christians choose to follow the pathway which truth illuminates even when it is hard—*especially* when it is hard. Truth telling matters: racism is alive and well in America. Daily headlines and news stories reveal and reinforce this fact. Our faith communities and adoptive families reflect the entire gamut of cultural and social attitudes about race, racism, and appropriate counterbalancing measures. Unless we consciously strive to expose, explore, unmask, and overturn racist biases, prejudices, and assumptions, they will occur in our faith communities.

Leslie Booker's presentation, "Embodying Radical Presence: Awareness of Race, Culture, and Self in Healing Trauma" issues a call for people to consider the result of dismissing the impact of racism: "Imagine if your experience was negated. That something that you knew to be true about yourself, your humanity, you're told that it wasn't true, or that it might be your imagination.[83] Can you imagine that happening for generation, after generation, after generation?" Imagine instead, what might happen if we "Lean towards this experience, so we could have greater understanding of how some folks move through this world, so that we could ally, so that we could be a friend, so that we could be a comrade to this person....The simple act of acknowledging that something has happened is an act of love and care, of turning towards our own humanity and our vulnerability."[84]

Booker's invitation to "radical presence" mirrors Christ's call to radical love and reminds us that we have a two-fold obligation as Christians. First, "To love our neighbor as we love ourselves." Second, to reflect the servant leadership of Christ that acknowledges truth and commits to bringing forth a world steeped in Christian values. The Church's responsibility to address racism is magnified because of its history and continuing efforts to pro-

---

[83] Leslie Booker. SoundsTrue.com. Embodying Radical Presence: Awareness of Race, Culture, and Self in Healing Trauma.

[84] Leslie Booker. Op cit.

mote transracial adoption. This has increased the presence of transracial adoptees in our pews.

On a Sunday morning in her congregation Sally can count on her hands the number of people of color sitting in the pew, one being her child. Overall, individual worship communities in America typically represent one color. According to The Pew Research group "…eight-in-ten American congregants still attend services at a place where a single racial or ethnic group comprises at least 80% of the congregation…"[85]

A majority of adopted children are nonwhite, yet a majority (73%) are adopted into white families. 63% of children adopted from foster care have white parents. The percentage goes up for children adopted in the United States (71%) and even higher for children adopted internationally (92%).[86]

It would follow that the congregations where adoptive families with children of color worship often are not very diverse. The reasons can be many. The adoptive family may prefer to remain in their home congregation because they feel deeply connected to the congregants from whom they can derive support. The worship practices and theology of the congregation may fit with their own understanding of faith. Many times, the faith community introduced the idea

---

[85] http://www.pewresearch.org/fact-tank/2014/12/08/many-u-s-congregations-are-still-racially-segregated-but-things-are-changing-2/

[86] https://aspe.hhs.gov/report/adoption-usa-chartbook-based-2007-national-survey-adoptive-parents/race-ethnicity-and-gender

of adoption to the parents so the adoptive parents may presume their children of color will be welcomed within this home community. They also may presume this will ensure their children will not encounter racism within this familiar community. Sadly, sometimes their actual experience contradicts their expectation.

Some adoptive parents may wish for a more diverse congregation, but their racially homogeneous community lacks that choice. Whatever the cause, the reality is that many of our children look at others around them and see very little of themselves reflected in their faith community.

Imagine you are a person of color sitting with your family in church waiting for the service to begin. Look around. Notice that only two other people are also persons of color. One of them is your brother. The other is a child, like you, adopted by a white family. Would you immediately feel like you belong? How might this very observable difference affect your state of mind, mood, and behavior?

Next, remember a time when you faced a circumstance in which you felt like an outsider and yet you had to stay, e.g., a work-connected event. Now imagine you knew your presence was merely being tolerated instead of fully welcomed. How did it tax you emotionally and physically? How quickly did you manage to escape? How eager were you to repeat the activity?

"Jane," a mother of transracially adopted children, reflects, "For we who are white, it may be difficult to understand what an impact a white faith community can have on our children of color especially if this community is unaware of its potential biases and blind spots. What we are naming here is white privilege—the luxury of having the culture around us respond to life from the experience which reflects our own personal experience—that of being white. The way we experience and order our world is honored and held by our culture as "the" way. This is white privilege at its core. These blind spots and biases that arise from the culture viewing all experience through a white lens give way to microaggressions."

When we exist in a homogenous bubble it is easy to presume that others experience a similar range of opportunity and expectations. We also assume that our preferences are the "correct" ones because we are more comfortable with them. We feel at home with the status quo, like we belong. We resist the discomfort of stretching to include an expanded and inclusive paradigm.

Jane shared her family's church experience. She and her husband adopted transracially with all their children being people of color.

"In our family, we always talked about the fact that Christ was not white, but had darker skin and probably was black. It's been a problem that Christ is depicted as white because [my kids] are not reflected at all. My daughter was six when we dropped her off for Sunday school one day. When I picked her up the teacher told me that my daughter, "Mary," had created a "problem" during class. The teacher said, 'Mary insisted the picture of Christ in the hallway is wrong, that Christ wasn't white. I told her she was wrong. Jesus was white."

Jane directed the teacher to resources that would show that Jesus was, indeed, not white.[87] Then she smiled at her daughter, got in the car, drove home, and never returned. This is another example of how racial bias and lack of adoption-attunement can damage the relationship between adoptees and their faith communities.

What Jane described to us are microinvalidations and microaggressions—everyday behaviors that, often without knowing, minimize or completely erase the realities of people of color. Sometimes they can be considered compliments by the giver:

To an international adoptee: *Wow, you speak English really well!*

To an African-American male: *Congratulations on making it through high school without getting into trouble!*

To an adoptive family with children of color: *Don't worry, we don't look at color here.*

To adoptive parents: *Can we have your child speak to the Sunday school about being black?* or, *We want to look more diverse, can we have your child on the front page of our website?*

In addition to comments such as these, microinvalidations and microaggressions can occur during sermons, in our Sunday school curriculum, and on our walls. If our children of color look around them in the church building and see only pictures of white people in the pictures on the walls and only white children in their Sunday school mate-

---

[87] http://www.christianitytoday.com/ct/2016/april/why-jesus-skin-color-matters.html

rials, they may fail to see themselves in the story of God's love and grace. Advocate Leslie Booker asserts that, "To those who are being transgressed against, there is no such thing as a micro-aggression. They feel quite macro."[88]

These everyday slights, put-downs, and minimizations are detrimental to our children's health. In fact, one study revealed that people who experienced microaggressions had feelings of sadness, anger, lower self-esteem, anxiety, and doubt that increased their stress. Even more alarming, the experiences had the potential of having a lasting impact on their lives.[89] In the Healing Trauma Summit 2018, Leslie Booker elaborated, "Our nervous system reacts to prejudice, discrimination, and inequity as a matter of survival because they are an assault on our fundamental sense of safety and right to exist in this world."[90]

There is another layer to white privilege: people of color often feel invisible. "Lolita," a transracial adoptee who was adopted at an older age reflects on the expectations imposed on her as a foster child. These expectations created a feeling of being "othered," objectified, and invisible.

---

[88] Leslie Booker. SoundsTrue.com. Embodying Radical Presence: Awareness of Race, Culture, and Self in Healing Trauma.

[89] The What, the Why, and the How: A Review of Racial Microaggressions Research in Psychology. https://www.ncbi.nlm.nih.gov/pmc/articles/PMC4762607/

[90] Leslie Booker. SoundsTrue.com. Embodying Radical Presence: Awareness of Race, Culture, and Self in Healing Trauma.

> *"Sunday is where you put on perfection. There is pride in how well the foster or adoptive parent cleaned the child up. But, no one ever came up to me and asked 'how are you doing with this family and with us [this church community] ...people assumed I was fragile and that the family was the protecting force. Sometimes people didn't even look at me."*
> —Lolita

People of color can become a canvas on which to paint our expectations of how things *ought* to look, how someone ought to be and act in order to belong. The pressure can be immense for adoptees or foster children when they are seen for who others want them to be rather than for who they really are. It can be exhausting for children as they attempt to figure out the unwritten and unspoken expectations that they must meet in order to be accepted in the community. At the same time their attempts will not result in full inclusion unless the congregation has done work around white privilege and is adoption-attuned.

Lolita reflects,

> *"I had to come to church and be fake, dress a certain way, put together even when I felt broken inside."*—Lolita

Children adopted into families who share their race or ethnicity can determine for themselves when or if they wish to reveal their adopted status; transracial adoptees do not have the same luxury of respite from this public state of otherness. Transracial adoptees cannot step out of their race. It is an integral part of their identity which they want to be respected, valued, and seen, not rendered invisible. In a parallel of the blessing of being heard, the blessing of being seen is also indistinguishable from being loved.

As Lolita suggests, a simple caring question from a church member, *How are you?* or *How are you doing with us and your family? I'm glad you are here!* can demonstrate to transracial adoptees that we see them for who they are. This can make all the difference. It can shift the power even a bit—from the society, The Church, and the adoptive family to the child.

Racism and white privilege also may affect the entire adoptive family. Because the parents are white, we may expect these parents to see their families and their faith in the same way we white folks do. We may expect their families to act like we do, to believe like we do, and to behave like we do. We may become colorblind and see only the whiteness of the family.

We may look primarily at how the family can fit into our community rather than how we are changed because of their fellowship with us—or how we should change to accommodate this diversity. This may be true especially with parishioners who have been with us for many years and now are new adoptive parents. Of course, the flip side of claiming only the commonalities is the devaluing of the differences.

"Any chance you have to make an adoptee feel like they

belong—grab it." —Megan D.

Faith communities ought to be, at their core, places where the experience of one becomes the experience of all. To create a genuine experience of belonging our "pegboards" must include many-shaped holes to accommodate and reflect those who are now members of our families and our faith community.

Putting ourselves in other people's shoes is a way faith communities and organizations can be a "family" to the adoptive and first families among us. It is a way to honor, elevate, and "see" adoptees of color and their families as unique and worthy of our listening, caring, and open conversation. To guide our actions, we can simply imagine if the circumstances were reversed. How would we hope the family, congregation, or community would treat us? Make that our template.

Even better than simply imagining our being in such a situation, we can seek out opportunities in which we actually are the minority person—not like a field trip to an exotic location—but as an act of solidarity with our children of color. This is not a once-and-done effort. Make it a routine part of our lives. Shop at stores and dine in restaurants in neighborhoods that include a majority of people of color.

By personally experiencing opportunities to be the minority, we can gain valuable insight into the lives of our children of color. This will sensitize us to their lived experience and open our eyes to the incidence of micro-aggressions, hostility, and scrutiny which are part of their daily lives. Keep in mind, however, that such short-term experiences as a minority can only hint at what our kids are actually living. They rarely get a chance to step out of their minority status.

For us adoptive parents especially, the relationship with our children should not be the first relationship that we have with people of color. Develop genuine friendships with people from many backgrounds, ethnicities, and races. Both we and our children will benefit. Be a contributor as well as a beneficiary of these cross-cultural relationships. It is vital to engage with people from our children's race and/or culture. As parents we want to ensure that they have time to be part of the activities and the communities where they are part of the majority.

Blissful ignorance is a disservice to our kids. Create an understanding that convinces them that you want to know what they are facing. The presence of a Caucasian parent provides a small degree of insulation from racism, although it certainly does not eliminate it entirely. Nor can we generalize that the positive way people react to our transracially adopted children when we are present also carries over to when we are not present. When transracial adoptees are out in the world alone, this mitigating force is absent. They are more vulnerable to the effects of racial discrimination, bias, and hate.

We must believe their reports and learn from their experiences. Hammer out a solution to this issue together. Ask them how you can best support them. This requires courage as well as a hard commitment to Jesus' call to action. Our strategies must advance beyond good intentions, move beyond the comfort of the status quo. We must support and advocate for change, and actively work to bring it about. Make a rigorous assessment of any biases about "those kinds of people" which enter our thoughts. Make a conscious effort to eliminate bias and prejudice within ourselves and our families.

Be an **"I stand-er"** and not a bystander. Speak out. Stand up.

Encourage dialogue within our churches and communities about these issues so that transracial adoptees feel it is safe to report microaggressions whether we are present or not. Discussion of white privilege and racism takes courage. It demands a willingness to set aside the familiarity and comfort of assumptions and presuppositions to honestly examine these topics. Brave conversations like these can only occur in a place where all feel valued, respected, and safe.

> *"White churches have got to start looking at our role in systemic racism in this country in real ways and become a part of dismantling that... and not just talk. We also need to be open in our prayers, sermons, and discussions about the social experiences and racial bias experiences in our communities."* —Jane.

It is important that faith communities consider these questions and explore them together.[91]

How are people of color faring in your area?

What roadblocks have been identified for people of color?

---

[91] https://www.npr.org/sections/codeswitch/2018/03/02/589483471/how-segregation-shapes-fatal-police-shootings?utm_source=facebook.com&utm_medium=social&utm_campaign=npr&utm_term=nprnews&utm_content=20180302

What appears on the walls, among the toys, in the books?
How diverse is the staff?
What is being preached and taught?
How do our policies and procedures reflect our awareness of white privilege and microaggressions?

It's time for us to look around our buildings, in our sanctuaries, fellowship halls, nurseries, classrooms, and staff to talk about racism and to educate members, volunteers and staff.

When we are serious about welcoming all adoptees and their families into our faith communities, we will be compelled to take off the blinders and look at adoptees of color and their families as individuals. We will see their color and pay attention to how we receive the children and their families. We will be moved to make changes because the way we express this welcoming spirit is through actions that create a feeling of welcome, and respect and honor the human family.

Some may argue that this is tokenism. However, when it comes from a place of love and belonging it will not be tokenism, but inclusion. We must be willing to hold the difficult conversations, admit and address bias, and engage in efforts to effect change. When we do so, it will be Christ's love in action through us. Adoptees will know that they are "home" in God's house and will feel like full members of His family.

> *"Up until the last couple of years, it [church] was terrible. I always felt judged and looked down upon. Now I have a great church family behind me."* —Anonymous

In an article titled, *Discussion on Race Offers Church a Second Chance to Take a Stand*, Fr. Joseph Brown, a Jesuit priest, suggests that faith communities must "embrace difference over conformity."[92] The article reported, "Rev. Darryl Gray, a Baptist minister described how people of color had lost faith in the church 'because we haven't seen you lately.' They weren't angry at the church, just disappointed that it hadn't reflected the one [actively striving for social justice] that their grandparents talked about, he said....Our young folk say even by being here tonight, they say we're trying to give the church another chance,' Gray told those gathered in the St. Alphonsus gymnasium. 'So, we have an opportunity, as well as an obligation to let them know that we are the church that Christ intended us to be.'"[93]

The Church can grab this "second chance" and step away from a narrow palette for depicting and defining group identity. Expand to include and value diversity. Rev. Gray advises that we must "pray with our feet," move beyond discussion, and engage in actions that bring our words to life and reflect Christ's radical love.

A song heard in churches all over America reminds us that "Jesus loves the little children. Red and yellow black and white, they are precious in His sight."[94] This song

---

[92] https://www.ncronline.org/news/justice/discussion-race-offers-church-second-chance-take-stand

[93] https://www.ncronline.org/news/justice/discussion-race-offers-church-second-chance-take-stand

[94] https://www.biblegateway.com/passage/?search=Matthew+19%3A14&version=NIV

echoes Matthew 19:14 where Jesus welcomes and loves children. Of course, He also welcomes and loves them as adults. We are called to do the same. "The King will answer and say to them, 'Truly I say to you, to the extent that you did it to one of these brothers of Mine, even the least of them, you did it to Me. "[95]

Questions to Consider

1. How can Matthew 25:40 inspire a commitment to motivate us to labor for social justice?
2. How does an emphasis on relationship as a higher priority than compliance help nurture belonging?
3. How does "color blindness" miss the mark in helping people feel welcome, respected, and valued?
4. How can we open our eyes to our own personal biases and then work to shift to a more inclusive point of view—and action?

Steps to Take

1. Assess your own thoughts and actions for any historical or current behaviors that reflect exclusion, racism, or insensitivity to social justice.

---

[95] http://biblehub.com/matthew/25-40.htm, New American Standard Bible

2. Commit to eliminating these biases within yourself, your congregation, and your community.

3. Speak up when people around you engage in discrimination or blindness to issues of social justice. Avoid dismissing, minimizing or denying their stories of personally experienced racism.

4. Imagine yourself as a member of an "othered" community, e.g., an adoptee, a person of color, a person locked into generational poverty. How would you want people to respond? Start taking these actions.

5. Embrace color equality not color blindness. People want to be seen as themselves, not rendered invisible.

CHAPTER 11

How We Can Help When Trauma Comes to Church

"And now these three remain: faith, hope and love. But the greatest of these is love."[96]

As we noted in previous chapters, adoptees' lives include a traumatic event—the separation from their first families. Trauma also occurs for the first family. They, too, have lost a family member. Adoptive parents also may experience trauma—from infertility to caregiver fatigue, and

---

[96] 1 Corinthians 13 New International Version (NIV)

secondary trauma[97]—and other life events not necessarily connected to adoption.

Whatever the case may be, our congregations consist of members who have heart wounds. These wounds call for special attention within churches. We are called to love with the deep love of Christ, a love that expands to include those who have great needs.

A huge gap exists between telling people they are welcomed and creating the experience of being welcomed. When we take even one step toward Christ's inclusive love, we will be changed and our hearts will be open not only to those in the adoption circle, but also to all who long to belong. Adoption-connected trauma is not the only way trauma comes to church. It appears in a variety of forms: from abusive relationships, disease and addictions, PTSD, personal and community experienced violence. Many of the techniques and changes we propose in this chapter will help address trauma regardless of how it originated.

When churches base their ministry on a Christ-like love that is sensitive to those with trauma, The Church will change. In 2015 Sally's congregation embarked on becoming a trauma-informed congregation. The suggestions made in this chapter are borne out of the study and intentional work of the congregation that she and her husband serve.

---

[97] Secondary trauma arises from a deep empathy for a child's past to the point where the parent experiences trauma themselves. High emotion and drama tend to occur when people struggle to heal and/or ignore trauma.

The urban congregation sits in the heart of Minneapolis. Among its members are adoptive children and families, families of mixed-race heritage, first mothers, families of divorce and blended families, single adults, widows and widowers, and traditional families. The neighborhood consists of a variety of faiths, cultures, and economic levels. As you would find in any congregation, trauma abounds.

Through its study on trauma, the faith community Sally serves discovered that many people who have been traumatized need unconditional love and acceptance for who they are. We can create fertile soil for the healing of trauma when we place connection before the "shoulds" and the "oughts."

The belief that God's unconditional love through Christ forms the foundation for all activity undergirds all the changes in Sally's congregation. Relationship above all else drives the decisions and life of the congregation. Influence or requirements in order to belong are not the motivating forces in the church.

Although this is easy to say, it is difficult to do. Over the centuries, churches have made requirements and influence primary goals. Handing down the faith, instilling solid morals in our children, directing both children and adults in the way they should act—all these are done in the hopes that we will produce good Christian people for the sake of the world and to the glory of God. While these goals are important, they are secondary and cannot be the purpose for existing. Making God's love known is primary. Relationship is primary.

Andrew Solomon, in his book, *Far from the Tree*, introduces the concepts of vertical and horizontal relationships. "Because of transmission of identity from one generation to the next, most children share at least some traits with their parents. These are vertical identities. Attributes and values are passed down from parent to child across the generations not only through strands of DNA but also through shared cultural norms. Ethnicity, for example, is a vertical identity...Religion is moderately vertical: Catholic parents will tend to bring up Catholic children, although the children may turn irreligious or convert to another faith. ...Often, however, someone has an inherent or acquired identity from a peer group. This is a horizontal identity. Such horizontal identities may reflect recessive genes, random mutations, prenatal influences, or values and preferences that a child does not share with his progenitors."[98]

Vertical relationships can communicate to people that they are not okay, loved, or accepted as they are. In the context of faith communities, requirements, proper instruction, acceptable behavior—all are in place so that members will adhere to the faith and so that the faith will be preserved. These goals are important, yet they need to be secondary. Just as Jesus adhered to his Jewish faith, He subordinated it to His goal of bringing salvation and love to all. Jesus illustrates a focus on love rather than on law at the conclusion of the story of the Good Samaritan. There Jesus

---

[98] Solomon, Andrew. Far from the Tree: Parents, Children, and the Search for Identity. Scribner. New York

asks the man, "What is written in God's law? How do you interpret it?"

He said, "That you love the LORD your God with all your passion and prayer and muscle and intelligence—and that you love your neighbor as well as you do yourself."

"Good answer!" said Jesus. "Do it and you will live."[99]

Solomon asserts that what people with challenges or those with trauma really need are "horizontal" relationships, ones that focus on acceptance and love. Faith communities who welcome people as who they are and love them where they happen to be fulfill Jesus' command to love one another. Indeed, traumatized people are sensitized to those who try to fix them, make them into something else, or get them to a certain point. We could say that as a community of God's children, The Church wants to promote horizontal relationships above vertical relationships.

Gregory Boyle, S.J. renowned community activist and author writes, "We sometimes let our preference for the poor [or otherwise marginalized,] to morph into a preference for the well-behaved and the most likely to succeed."[100]

Congregations that focus on horizontal relationships will pay attention to the ways they can include, rather than exclude. They will focus on the radical, inclusive love of

---

[99] Message Bible, E. Peterson. Copyright @2002 by Eugene Peterson. Navpress Luke 10:26b-28

[100] Boyle, Gregory, Tattoos on the Heart, Free Press, 2010, page 179

Christ rather than the requirements to belong.[101] In his book, *Tattoos on the Heart*," Quoting child psychiatrist Alice Miller, Fr. Gregory Boyle writes, "We choose to become...'"enlightened witnesses"—people who through their "kindness, tenderness, and...focused attentive love return folks to themselves. It is a returning—not a measuring up...we seek to tell each person this truth: they are exactly what God had in mind when God made them.'"[102]

Sally's congregation embarked on creating this fundamental paradigm shift. First, it set out to make God's unconditional love through Christ the foundation for all activity in the congregation by modifying its vision and mission to reflect its commitments. The result was the vision: *Building Relationships with Christ and Each Other* and the mission: *By Engaging the Community in Hope, Healing, and Wholeness*. Although the congregation still seeks to share the Christian faith and beliefs with members and friends, making someone to be a certain way or behave a certain way is not the ultimate goal.

Their new purpose has created changes on every level of the congregation. The change began where it needed to begin, at the root of the congregation's ministry—its constitution. They modified their by-laws to reduce the requirements for membership. In its by-laws the congregation now acknowledges people who may consider themselves

---

[101] Solomon, Andrew. Far from the Tree: Parents, Children, and the Search for Identity. Scribner. New York

[102] Boyle, ibid. page 192

members or connected to the congregation even though they are not actively involved or may never have stepped into the church building. This has implications for funerals at the church. If a grieving family calls and says that they would like to have the funeral service of their loved one at the church because they once attended a potluck there, the congregation does not first determine if the person or the family is a member.

The by-laws go further. The congregation will not assume that someone does not want to be a member any longer if they are inactive for a certain period of time. The congregation no longer automatically removes them from membership. Instead, the congregation reaches out to members after a certain period of time to continue the connection. Only if a member initiates removal from membership will they be taken off "the rolls."

To be certain these foundational changes create a messier record of who actually is a part of the congregation. Keeping track of people becomes more difficult and the true nature of active members may be clouded. For instance, a congregation may have 500 people listed as members, but only 200 active members. In the end, why does it really matter? When relationship is central, who is in and who is out becomes a low priority.

You may wonder how your congregation can begin this process. First, secure a commitment to this paradigm shift from core members of the congregation and its leadership. Their "buy in" is essential. We suggest that you offer this book to your pastoral team and church lay leadership and then gather them together for a time of discernment and prayer. Ask the group: Is the church committed to putting relationships first, to creating a safe place and ministry for the traumatized or excluded? If the commitment is present, create study and discernment groups throughout the congregation to discuss trauma. This book is an excellent resource for understanding what happens to people when they have experienced any life-altering event. Its usefulness is not limited to addressing adoption trauma.

Once you have a solid portion of the congregation aware and committed to change, then you are ready to develop vision and mission statements that reflect the emphasis on relationship-building purely for the sake of people's well-being. Invite all groups in the congregation to reflect on how their group supports the new mission statement of the church.

Review your constitution (if you have one) or operating documents of the congregation and revise them where necessary so that they align with your new focus. Policies such as qualifications/requirements for membership most likely need work. If you have a process for discipline that leads to removal of membership, consider developing a process for renewal of the relationship. This might be reinstatement of active membership or a more distant relationship. This may be as simple as a commitment of the congregation to pray for these members.

After your congregation has secured a church-wide commitment to focusing on relationship as its core mission, you are ready to reflect these beliefs in every aspect of congregational life. Below are just some of ways the paradigm shift created new approaches throughout the congregation Sally serves. They are intended as food to fuel your own changes within your congregation.

Make Changes and Enhancements to Your Physical Space to Encourage Relationship

• Set the tables in the fellowship hall in larger groupings to encourage family-style instead of cafeteria-style meals. It's amazing what can happen when we pass the plate and have to ask our neighbor to pass the butter!

• Have fellowship/coffee time take place closer to the worship space to encourage a fluid transition from one location to the next. If you can, have the coffee hour in different areas of the building to encourage others to participate. For example, if you have an elevator and there is space, have coffee available near the elevator, as well. Another example: occasionally have coffee and snacks in the education area, encouraging folks to go to the youth and hang in their "neck of the woods."

• Provide a rocking chair in the sanctuary for young parents or those who might have anxiety.

• Establish a quiet corner close to worship that is inviting for use when a child may need less stimulation.

• Increase entryway space if it's small to allow for movement.

• Consider the positioning of the pews. Is there any other way they can be configured to encourage community and relationship building? If you can, remove some pews and provide standing tables for those who find it difficult to sit or need an opportunity to move due to any medical condition, including anxiety or fear of crowded spaces. For some who have experienced trauma, knowing they can leave quickly allows them to be able to come to worship and stay for the duration of the service.

• Paint calming colors on the walls.

• Have colorful plants outside of the building.

• Notice the temperature in the building and make adjustments so it is comfortable.

• To ensure the safety of children and to protect adults from false accusations, comply with the safety rules set forth by your denomination or insurance company.

Practical Changes

• Provide a "fidgets cart" near the worship space or fidget bags draped over the pews or chairs in the worship space where people young and old can reach in for a squeeze ball, stuffed animal, scented PlayDoh© (there are homemade recipes on line that make a lesser-scented dough to which you can add aromatherapy oils), etc..

• Equip a pew with coloring crayons, paper, etc., directly on the pew/chair where a child can kneel on the floor and use the pew/chair as a table.

• Provide brief explanations in the bulletin/order of service that frame the various elements in the light of their healing qualities.

Examples:

- Confession and Forgiveness- Here we let go of our disappointments and failures of the week, trusting in God's ability to 'remember our sins no more' so our here-and-now will not be clouded by our past and our future can be open to possibility.

- Service of the Word— Hearing God's love and guidance and listening to the Word, we find meaning in our experiences and move forward with faith and confidence.

- Prayers— Together we lift up our joys and concerns. By doing so we grow as a God-formed community and we are reminded that we are not alone.

- Hymns— Singing together reminds us that we all have a place in the choir; we all are important to the Body of Christ in our own, unique way. Christ's body in this world is enhanced through our collective voices.

- Write additional liturgy for dedication and baptism such as:

    ¤ Invite and include a space for first families. If they cannot be present, acknowledge their "presence" in the child's life and their importance to the growth of the child. Have a prayer for first families. (See a sample in the Appendix.)

In whatever you do your foundational commitment to be joined in community as an embodiment of God's love drives the changes you make. Strive to build connection, to eliminate judgment, and to increase a sense of personal belonging. In doing so, you will be a potential participant in the healing of a sibling in Christ. You may be amazed at the way your congregation grows in vitality, faithfulness, and spiritual depth because you have embraced the radical love of Christ Jesus in the entire life of the congregation.

Fr. Boyle defines our job description as Christians to seek kinship and "remembering that we belong to one another, and letting souls feel their worth."[103]

Questions to Consider

1. What are the benefits of becoming a trauma-informed congregation?

2. While indoctrination in the faith is important, what are the benefits of placing primary emphasis on relationship and belonging?

3. How does the physical space of a church contribute to the creation of connection between its congregants?

4. How does reframing behavior as the language of trauma open possibilities for healing?

---

[103] Boyle, ibid. page 196

Conclusion

Reimagining Adoption makes a provocative conclusion that reflects the radical, restorative love of Christ: congregations must promote healthy communities and support struggling families to avoid family fracture in the first place. When adoption is necessary this book will equip readers with a heart-centered approach to serve adoptees and their families and to show them that they are loved, valued, and important to us—and to God.

Adoptee voices woke us and you from "sleep" and called us to be courageous, compassionate witnesses. Adoption-attunement calls us to stay awake in a way that the disciples failed to do when Jesus pleaded with them to watch while he prayed in the Garden of Gethsemane. Love and good intentions alone cannot fully meet the needs of adoptees and their families, so we asked you to stand as compassionate witnesses, open wide the circle and enfold them as brothers and sisters in Christ.

Mindful of the words of Isaiah 40, "Comfort ye, comfort ye my people, saith your God,"[104] we now call you to a leadership role. Spread the awareness of Adoption-attunement. Commit to actions that preserve families and validate their reality. Engage in efforts to bring about social justice. Declare the hand of God not only in the fracture of vulnerable families, but also in ministry to them. When adoption occurs, be the channel of divine love and healing by supporting the adoption constellation with compassion and validation.

An adoption-attuned approach can help heal the wounds of adoption and nurture the sense of belonging desired by all human beings. We believe our assertions are sound and genuinely reflect Christian values of faith, hope, and love. We see our call to re-envision the relationship between faith and adoption fundamentally as a call to love and to serve God through our service to others.

We hope readers will agree and will lift up this message and spread it far and wide. Consider this quote from the website AdoptionMuseumProject.Org, "We can see both the big picture and the personal stories and how it is all connected…this kind of inquiry can help move us towards ensuring justice and dignity for all involved in adoption… Changing adoption so that it values all people involved,

---

[104] https://www.biblegateway.com/passage/?search=Isaiah+40&version=KJV

begins with noticing. When it helps and when it harms. The whole story."[105]

A truth rings out: regardless of how we look on the outside or what tragedies and traumas have shaped us, none of us is a "mistake." Each of us has been created in God's image. In faith we seek answers to the universal questions: Who Am I? With Whom and Where Do I Belong? At its core this also is the task of faith communities, to make sure that people know who they are and whose they are.

"He will answer them, 'I'm telling the solemn truth: Whenever you failed to do one of these things to someone who was being overlooked or ignored, that was me—you failed to do it to me."

Matthew 25:45[106]

---

[105] http://adoptionmuseumproject.org/our-perspective/

[106] https://www.biblegateway.com/verse/en/Matthew%2025:45

Acknowledgments

A book requires the collaboration of many people. We are grateful for the support and patience of our families, the encouragement and wisdom of our colleagues at GIFT— Susan David and Joann DiStefano. We thank all of the folks who read draft after draft, critiqued our words, and reviewed the manuscript. Your insight and commentary made a difference.

Dan Ankerfelt participated in the process from start to finish. His perspective as a pastor and an adoptive parent proved exceptionally valuable. Thank you, Dan, for your patience, commitment, and suggestions.

We send our appreciation to Deb Reisner for her input on White Privilege, to Beverly Ankerfelt, Shirley Smith and Linda Lightsey Rice for their editorial expertise, and to Brooke Randolph, LMHC, for providing an adoption therapist's evaluation of the manuscript.

We are especially indebted to Lynn Grubb. In many ways, she has been a midwife to this project. Our conversations with her galvanized us to move from, "We should write a book," to actually putting in the time and energy to create this book and then make it shine.

We also gratefully acknowledge Sherrie Eldridge, voice *par excellence* for adoptees, for her generous infusion of insight, encouragement, and expertise. We thank Anne Heffron, author and adoptee activist who vouched for us; her unflagging encouragement helped us connect with adult adoptees who were willing to share their stories with us. Her encouragement and wisdom inspired us.

We offer heartfelt thanks to the many adoptees and first mothers who shared their stories so eloquently. We hope you feel that we have honored your trust in us. Without your input this book would have been impossible.

Appendix

The Adoptees Bill of Rights
—Author Unknown

1. We have the right to dignity and respect.
2. We have the right to know we are adopted.
3. We have the right to possess our original birth certificate.
4. We have the right to possess all of our adoption records.
5. We have the right to full knowledge of our origins, ethnic and religious background, our original name and any pertinent medical and social details.
6. We have the right to updated medical and social history of our birthparents.
7. We have the right to personal contacts with each of our birth families as do all other humans.
8. We have the right to live without guilt toward any set of parents.

9. We have the right to treat and love both sets of parents as one family.

10. We have the right and obligation to show our feelings.

11. We have the right to become whole and complete people.

12. We have a right and obligation not to violate the dignity of all people involved in the adoption triad and to carry our message to all adopted children who still suffer.[107]

---

[107] www.americanadoptioncongress.org/adoptee_rights.php

The Birth Parents Bill of Rights

Author Unknown

1. We have the right to dignity and respect.
2. We have the right to know if our surrendered child is alive and well.
3. We have the right to possess, surrender, relinquishment, consent to adopt, termination of parental rights and hospital records pertaining to ourselves and our child.
4. We have the right and obligation to provide full knowledge to our child of their origins, ethnic and religious backgrounds, their original name and any pertinent medical and social details.
5. We have the right to personal contact with our adult child, as all other humans. We have the right to update our medical and social history for our child.
6. We have the right to live without guilt toward our child. We have the right to give back or let go of any shame caused by our pregnancy and our child's adoption.
7. We have the right to love our child as all other parents. We have the right and obligation to show our feelings.
8. We have the right to become whole and complete people. We have the right and obligation not to violate the dignity of all people in the adoption circle and to

carry our message to all birth parents who still suffer.[108]

---

[108] www.americanadoptioncongress.org/adoptee_rights.php

Prayers, Liturgies, and Family Rituals for Wholeness and Belonging

The elements of worship and ceremony in the church reflect our beliefs about God as well as God's children. For those of us who have grown up in a congregation we may not be as aware of the subtle ways our forms of worship can influence how we feel about ourselves and others. However, it is important that the prayers and liturgies we offer reflect the all-encompassing love of God through Christ.

These enhancements to the dedication or baptismal rite do not alter foundational requirements; they offer a way of validating the grief and loss in which an adoption takes root. Prayers for days that may be difficult or complex for those in the adoption circle are also included.

We also include a placement ceremony. This is intended for use at the time the child is received into the arms of the adoptive parents. There is room in this ceremony to include foster parents as well. The goal is to give voice to the pain and joy of the day as well as to encircle the child with as many members of his/her "full" family as possible, (e.g., first, foster, adoptive relatives, or any person fulfilling an informal family relationship role.)

You have our permission to use these materials, or adapt them as you see fit with proper acknowledgment.

Baptism/Dedication:

- In your welcome include (if appropriate and after permission is granted) the name(s) of the first family. This could include as many first family members as possible.
- Invite the first family forward for the baptism or dedication as well as the adoptive family.
- Address both first and adoptive families as the promises are read. Example: Do you, [first family and adoptive family names] promise to raise this child in the faith, to show him/her the way to go and to teach them about the promises he/she receives today so that they he/she may grow to know and experience the love of God?
- Include in the prayer for the parents the names of the first mother and first father, if applicable. Example: Gracious God, send your help and love to [names of first family and adoptive family] as they care for this child. Make them teachers and examples of your love and care. Enfold them in your grace throughout their own lives so that they may have strength and joy for the journey ahead.
- Consider inviting commitment from the congregation that encourages understanding and acceptance rather than judgment. Example:

Children of [name of congregation], do you promise to help this new friend at church, showing her/him the way, being kind to her/him, and including her/him in children's activities? If so, say, "Yes!"

Adults of [name of congregation], Do you, those in the middle ages of your life, promise to walk with this family, showing them understanding and patience and helping them in the name of Christ? If so, answer, "Yes!"

Seniors of [name of congregation], Do you, with the wisdom of your years, promise to bring your strong faith to this child and the family, guiding them by your gentle love and reminding them that they have support and will be able to make it through with God's help? If so, answer, "Yes!"

- Consider creating an action for the first parent(s) as well as the adoptive parent(s) such as lighting a candle from two separate candles that represents the mutual commitment to the child and the joining of two families. (Refer to the placement ceremony for a possible source for the candles.)

Mother's Day Prayer

We pray for mothers we love and mothers we struggle to love, for first mothers, adoptive mothers, stepmothers, and foster mothers and for those who long to be mothers. We pray for those mothers whose children have died, for those whose children are missing, and for those whose children are estranged. We pray for all those who have nurtured and mothered us in the faith, be they female or male. Grant eternal rest to those mothers who have died. In God's grace we pray. AMEN.[109]

Father's Day Prayer

---

[109] Deacon Sue Arens, 2017

O Most High, may your steadfast love and faithfulness sustain your people. Bless all fathers and father figures in our lives with your love and faithfulness. Bless those who long to be fathers, and those whose fathers have died, are unknown, or are estranged. Bless families who are separated by distance, by physical needs, by memory impairment, and all for whom this day is difficult. Amen.[110]

Adoption Entrustment Ceremony

Presider
Today is a special day.
It is a day of passage for one of your children, [name].
We gather today to acknowledge the gifts of Life,
This Child,
Our commitment to one another,
And our love for [child's name].
We welcome all who are present to share and witness this moment with us
And remember all who have been a part of our journey.
We light two candles to represent
The two sets of parents this child will always have.
The first parents
Who will always remain in [child's name] heart and mind,
And who will always have [child's name] in their hearts and minds;

---

[110] Deacon Sue Arens, 2017

And the adoptive parent/s, [name of parent/s]

Who receive this child to live in their hearts and in their home.

We light a third candle to represent this child and the love that unites these parents. We encourage that this candle be used on this child's baptism/dedication day as a symbol of God's continued blessings and the "wholeness" of this child's life that is being recognized by us today.

There are others with you here today- [recite names, e.g., social worker, and others who may be gathered, such as other children] to share this important day with you.

[Add foster parents, if available]

We especially acknowledge the foster parents, [name(s)]

Who, through their nurturing and love for [name],

Have also become a part of the extended family

And the roots of his/her early life.

They, too, will let go of a unique role today that they have had in this child's life.

First family member speaks:

I, [name(s)] am your mother/father.

I am in awe that you have been born.

You are beautiful and perfect just as you are.

It takes all of my strength to let you go.

Difficult circumstances bring me to this excruciating decision.

It is not your fault.

I marvel at the fragileness of your life

And at the beauty you bring into this world,

With a heavy heart, I make this choice to be separated from you.

Your life has brought me joy

And will continue to bring it to so many.

Know how much I love you.

My desire to shelter and protect you leads me

To give this family to you

And to entrust you to them.

I have searched and found them.

I have met and liked them.

I have listened and learned that I can trust them.

Know that I never could and never will forget you.

You are now and always will be a part of my life.

My prayers will always be that you are safe and happy

And deeply loved.

First family addresses adoptive family:

[Names of adoptive parent(s)],

I entrust to you my precious child [name] whom I have received from God. Welcome her/him Love her. Support her.

Nurture into the fullness which God has designed her to become.

I wish her happiness in each day of her life.

May she know strength, resilience, understanding, empathy, joy, and love.

I know that there will be painful times in each person's life.

Be there to listen and share.

Cushion the hard times with your wisdom and your love.

Celebrate the milestones in her life.

Joy shared is joy multiplied,

So, frame these milestones with laughter and festivities, family and friends.

In times of difficulty, help shoulder her/his burdens

So (s)he does not bear them alone.

Share your compassion, your hope, and your faith

So that you can all recover and heal.

Share with me as your story of becoming a family unfolds

so that I may continue to be a part of my child's life.

Validate and have compassion for the loss that both my child and I face.

Hold space for my presence in her life.

Acknowledge and value our bond as a permanent tie that binds us for life.

Welcome me as an important part of her life journey even if only in spirit.

We are forever joined by our love for our child.

Adoptive family addresses the first family:

[name of first family member], we tenderly receive from you, this beautiful child, [name].

We know because of you, his/her life IS.

Today is a day full of so many emotions for us, too.

Our joy in becoming parents to [name of child] has no limits.

We acknowledge our happiness is rooted in your tears of grief and loss.

With you we feel your pain in letting go.

We are humbled by your trust in us,

And we commit ourselves to being the best parents we can become.

Know that we will pass on to [child's name] the story you have shared with us.

She will know how very much you have and will always love her.

All that we have shared together

And all that we have received from you is the foundation of her life.

We will continue marking this day in how we live our lives.

The pain that you have experienced we hold carefully in our hearts as an expression of your love.

The future may send us in separate directions from time to time in our journeys,

But, our love for [name of child],

Will be woven like a ribbon through our lives, binding us together

Until the circle of our love that we have begun with our sharing is completed.

[All speak together]
We ask God to bless one another and most especially,
We ask God to bless [name of child].
Today, for the sake of this beautiful child,
We commit to an Open Adoption agreement.
Before God and these witnesses,
We promise to forge a relationship of integrity and mutual respect
With the best interest of our child as its purpose.
When things get complicated or difficult,
We will strive to make it work.
We accept this relationship as a sacred covenant before God
And we will do our best to honor it.[111]

National Adoption Month Observance

In November National Adoption Month inspires a surge of pro-adoption events. Originally established as a way to encourage adoption of foster children, it has now become a celebration of adoption in general. It is important than any National Adoption Month events not lose sight of the grief and losses which underpin adoption.

The lighting of candles has a powerful role in cultural and faith efforts to dispel ignorance, bring hope, and illu-

---

[111] Adapted from Lutheran Social Services of Wisconsin

minate a path out of darkness. The flame of a candle symbolizes the glow of hope. We offer this sample ritual as an example of a balanced ceremony. It can be done in a church or alternate gathering place. It can even be held as a private family celebration. Adapt as necessary.*

Materials Needed:

Three candles—

> One to represent the birth family,
>
> One to represent the adoptive family,
>
> One to represent the faith family, adopted Family support group, or sponsoring organization. (Light this candle before the ritual begins.)
>
> > Water-filled pitcher
> >
> > Basin

Participants:

Leader (This can be a pastor, church elder, or any lay person)

Adopted child/ren

Adoptive parent(s)

First Family

Friends

Extended family

Faith community and or adoptive family support group

Script:

Guide: Point to the pre-lit candle and say:

This candle signifies us as a community who gather here today.

Together we are stronger, together we share our joys.

Adoption brings together children and families.

One family welcomes a new member with joy and grateful hearts.

At the same time another family loses a member and grieves that loss with heavy hearts. They are separated from one another but not forgotten.

Valued even if no longer present.

As part of today's observance, we honor first parents, the givers of life.

Whether we are adopted or not,

A part of them lives on in each of us.

I invite _____ (a designated adoptee who volunteered ahead of time,)

To come and light this candle to represent his/her first family.

Today we think also of children in foster care

For whom family reunification may not be possible.

We comfort them in this loss

And we raise up their hope of finding a family to enfold them.

Adopted child or adopted adult

Today I remember my first parents.

In their honor I light this candle. (Ignite it using the pre-lit community candle.)

Adoptive parent

Today I renew my commitment

To honor the sacred promise I made,

To raise my child with unconditional love,

To meet his needs, especially those resulting from his adoption,

To keep him safe,

To nurture and value his talents,

And to celebrate not only the ways he is like us,

But also, the ways in which his differences enrich our family.

First parent (if present)

While I miss my child's physical presence in my daily life,

I affirm that he is in my heart every day,

That I hope he will find happiness in his family,

And that he will know how much I love and care for him.

Readings (letters, poems, etc.)

Remember to acknowledge losses and gains, sadness and joy. This event should validate the experiences of adoptive and birth families, and give witness to their struggles. Encourage participants to freely express themselves and ensure they understand that this is a forum that recognizes and welcomes the full range of their experiences.

Conclusion

Include a song. Invite the group to clasp hands in a continuous loop while the **guide** says:

We stand as a community in support of one another,
Sharing joys, dividing sorrows,
And shouldering burdens.
May we remember to offer each other help and support.
May we have the courage to ask one another for help.
May we have the compassion to be that help.
We give thanks for the blessing of being part of each other's lives.

*When sharing this ceremony, please credit as follows:

Used with permission or, adapted from, *Reimagining Adoption: What Adoptees Seek from Families and Faith* by Sally Ankerfelt, M. Div. and Gayle H. Swift, CPC

Elements of Adoption-attunement

Consider grief and loss issues

Use sound adoption language

Understand the attachment process

Respect birth parents and first families

Model, teach, and hold healthy boundaries

Educate family, friends, teachers, and faith communities about adoption

Remember a child's story belongs to him

Recognize adoption as a family experience

Encourage playfulness and good humor as a family value

Integrate a child's birth heritage

Honor a child's need to know and connect with birth family

Nurture and value child's innate talents. Encourage them to be themselves

Recognize parents must work through their own grief and loss issues

Follow ethical practices

Operate with a child-centric focus[112]

---

[112] Gayle H. Swift with Casey A. Swift, *ABC, Adoption & Me: A Multicultural Picture Book for Adoptive Families*, WRB Publishing, 2013. Used with permission

Seven Core Issues of Adoption [113]

Rejection: Suffers fear of abandonment and feelings of not being good enough to stay with.

Loss: Experiences trouble holding on and letting go.

Guilt and Shame: Believes he/she does not deserve good fortune and struggles with anger.

> **Important distinctions:**
>
> > **Guilt** = "I did something bad."
> >
> > **Shame** = "I am bad."

Identity: Grapples with integrating all parts of himself. *Who am I? Where did I come from?*

Intimacy: May bond inappropriately—too soon, too late, too intensely, not at all—because fears loss, abandonments, rejection.

Mastery and Control: Realizes what adoption has done to him/her, feels powerless and seeks what control he/she can find.

---

[113] Adapted from a chart created by Brooke Randolph, LMHC with Kerrie Siegl and Barbara Freedgood. Entourage Publishing. 2011. Used with Permission

Grief: Unresolved grief can lead to depression and anger.

Additional Resources

Websites

The internet can be a marvelous resource for adoptive parents seeking adoption support services, as well as education for adoption related issues. We have compiled a list of resources for families who wish to learn more about adoption, the adoption process, and issues that affect families who have chosen adoption.

Adopt America Network —partners with hundreds of public and private organizations across the country, matching waiting children with eager families. (adoptamericanetwork.org)

Adoptee Rights Coalition — Adoptees lead this coalition of adoptees, original families, and adoptive families. They lobby for legislation that gives adult adoptee unconditional access to Original Birth Certificates. (Adopteerightscoalition.com)

Adoption.com — Contains a wide variety of adoption topics and resources for families. (adoption.com)

The Adoption Exchange — The Adoption Exchange recruits families for children who have survived abuse and neglect, supports adoptive families throughout every phase of the adoption process, and trains child welfare professionals. The Adoption Exchange maintains a national training presence, and connects children in eight member states CO, MO, NV, NM, OK, SD, UT and WY with American families living here and abroad.

Adoptioninformation.com — A resource for families considering adoption. It contains articles, resources and tips for people considering or those who already have adopted.

Adoption Institute — The Adoption Institute's mission is to provide leadership that improves adoption laws, policies and practices – through sound research, education and advocacy – in order to better the lives of everyone touched by adoption.

AdoptionMuseumProject.org — creates interactive museum experiences to help expand the understanding of adoption and to develop a commitment to justice issues associated with it.

AdoptUsKids — The mission of AdoptUsKids is two-fold: to raise public awareness about the need for foster and adoptive families for children in the public child welfare system; and to assist U.S. states, territories and tribes to recruit and retain foster and adoptive families and connect them. (AdoptUsKids.org)

America's Kids Belong — "Uniting government, faith-based, business and creative communities to end the foster care and adoption crisis in the U.S. – state by state." (americaskidsbelong.org)

American Adoption Congress — An international organization providing education to professionals and the adoption constellation. (americanadoptioncongress.org)

BeyondConsequences.com — Provides helpful articles and resources for adoptive parents

Bleedingheartsadoption.wordpress.com — a blog written by an adoptee/first mother/adoptee rights activist with a strong focus on the intersection between faith and adoption.

Dave Thomas Foundation for Adoption — This site provides adoption facts, information, free resources, myths and misrepresentations. They have an amazing links page that has to be visited. It is broken up into categories and is one of the most comprehensive links pages available. (davethomasfoundation.org)

Dream Makers Project – (dreammakersproject.org) — Funds opportunities for youth aging out of foster care.

Growing Intentional Families Together—Offers coaching services before, during, and after adoption. GIFT does not facilitate adoptions. All coaches are adoptive parents and certified professionals. Authors Sally Ankerfelt and Gayle Swift are two of the co-founders. (GIFTfamilyServices.com)

National Adoption Center — The National Adoption Center expands adoption opportunities for children living in foster care throughout the United States. It is a resource to families and to agencies who seek the permanency of caring homes for children.

National Child Welfare Resource Center for Adoption — Information to aid with special needs adoption programs as well as resources available through the NRCA. Also offered are web links to other helpful organizations and publications with a particular emphasis on working with special needs adoption. (NRCAdoption.org)

North American Council on Adoptable Children — Great resource for information on Title IV-E Adoption Assistance program for each state and Canadian province as well as comprehensive post-adoption support resources. (NACAC.org)

Partnership for Permanence—is also known as **P4P** — "an organization for former foster youth and adoptees coming together to raise awareness and actively work to improve the child welfare system." While their own personal experiences may have been imperfect, they have taken this experience and channeled it into a desire to help others. They use their personal insights about what helped them and what failed them to improve the experience for children currently in the foster care system. (partnershipsforpermanence.org)

fp365 — "Is a global family preservation movement. Our mission is to empower vulnerable, expectant mothers and prevent family separation. **fp365** is dedicated to building a strong foundation of advocates willing to provide local support, networking and community involvement." familypreservation365.com

Tapestry Books — This website specializes in books related to adoption for children, adults and professionals. It includes fiction and non-fiction. (tapestrybooks.com)

Together We Rise — Supports children in foster care. It spearheads three programs: *Sweet Cases* which provides duffle bags to replace trash bags, *Build A Bike* which provides bicycles to kids aging out of care, and the *Family Fellowship Scholarship Program* which provides scholarships to kids aging out of care.

Voice for Adoption — Voice for Adoption is a national collaboration of child welfare organizations whose mission is to speak with policy makers representing the interests of foster children awaiting adoption and the families who adopt them. (voice-for-adoption.org)

Blogs

Dear Adoption is a platform which shares a vast array of experiences as lived by those most affected by adoption: adoptees. **DA**, exists to elevate adoptee voices and shift the narrative surrounding adoption to better educate society. (DearAdoption.com)

Growing Intentional Families Together (GIFT Family Services) offers many resources to families before, during, and after adopting; it does not facilitate adoptions. A weekly blog is one of the many resources available on this website. (GIFTfamilyServices.com)

LavenderLuz.com — blog maintained by Lori Holden, author of *the Open-hearted Way to Open Adoption*. She is an adoptive parent and open adoption advocate. Her blog has won numerous awards and was named a Top Adoption Blogger by Adoptive Families magazine.

No Apologies for Being Me— blog written by activist, author and adoptee, Lynn Grubb about life as an adoptee. The site includes many excellent resources (noapologies-forbeingme.blogspot.com)

Portrait of an Adoption — curated by award-winning author and adoptive mom Carrie Goldman. Every November she features a roster of guest bloggers who represent the varying perspectives of the adoption constellation. (chicagonow.com/portrait-of-an-adoption)

Writing to Connect — reviews general interest books through an Adoption-attuned lens. Written by Gayle H. Swift, it outlines ways families can use books that are not directly about adoption to deftly raise adoption-sensitive topics. (GaylehSwift.com/blog)

Podcasts

Adoptees On hosted by adoptee Haley Radke features adult adoptees sharing their experiences and insights.

Adoption-attuned Parenting Essentials explores how parents can best relate and connect to their adopted child. GIFT coaches, Joann DiStefano and Susan David, share constructive tips and tools for building a strong foundation for adoptive families.

Suggested Reading for Adults

20 Things Adoptive Parents Need to Succeed: Discover the Unique Need of Your Adopted Child and Become the Best Parent You Can, Sherrie Eldridge

20 Things Adopted Kids Wish Their Adoptive Parents Knew, Sherrie Eldridge

Adoptee Survival Guide: Adoptees Share Their Wisdom and Tools, Lynn Grubb

Adopting the Hurt Child: Hope for Families with Special Needs Kids, A Guide for Parents and Professionals, Gregory Keck and Regina Kupecky

Adoption Is A Family Affair!, Patricia Irwin Johnston

Adoption Parenting: Creating a Toolbox, Building Connection, Jean MacLeod, Sheena Macrae, PhD.

The Adoptive & Foster Parent Guide: How to Heal Your Child's Trauma and Loss (Volume 1). Carol Lozier, LCSW

Attaching Through Love, Hugs and Play, Deborah D. Gray

Beyond Consequences, Logic & Control, Heather Forbes, LCSW

The Body Keeps Score, Bessel van der Kolk, M.D.

Brainstorm: The Power and Purpose of the Teenage Brain, Dan Siegel

The Connected Child, Karyn Purvis, Ph.D.

Connecting with Kids through Stories: Using Narratives to Facilitate Attachment in Adopted Children, Denise B. Lacher, et al

Dare to Love, Heather Forbes, LCSW

Dear Wonderful You, Letters to Adopted & Fostered Youth (The AN-YA Project), Diane Rene Christian

The Family of Adoption, Joyce Maguire Pavao

The Five Love Languages of Children, Gary Chapman, PhD. and Ross Campbell, MD.

Flip the Script: Adult Adoptee Anthology (The AN-YA Project) Paperback, 2015 by M. C. Maltempo (Author), Diane René Christian (Editor), Amanda H.L. Transue Woolston (Editor), Rosita González (Editor)

Help for Billy, Heather Forbes, LCSW

Hope for Healing: A Parent's Guide to Trauma and Attachment, Association for Training n Trauma and Attachment in Children (ATTACH), Paperback, 2001.

It's Not about You: Reunion, Search and Open Adoption, Brooke Randolph, LMHC.

Life Books: Creating a Treasure for the Adopted Child, Beth O'Malley, M.ED.

My Foster Care Journey, Beth O'Malley, M.ED.

The Newbie's Guide to Positive Parenting, Rebecca Eames

No Matter What, Sally Donovan

The Open-hearted Way to Open Adoption, Lori Holden with Crystal Hass

Perpetual Child: Adult Adoptee Anthology: Dismantling the Stereotype (The AN-YA Project), Diane René Christian (Author), Amanda H.L. Transue-Woolston (Editor)

ADDITIONAL RESOURCES

Reimagining Adoption: What Adoptees Seek from Families and Faith, Sally Ankerfelt, M. Div. and Gayle H. Swift
Telling the Truth to Your Adopted or Foster Child: Making Sense of the Past, Betsy Keefer & Jayne E. Schooler
Twenty Things Adopted Kids Wish Their Adoptive Parents Knew, Sherrie Eldridge
Unofficial Guide to Adoptive Parenting, Sally Donovan and Dr. Vivien Norris
The Unofficial Guide to Therapeutic Parenting—The Teen Years, Sally Donovan
You Don't Look Adopted, Anne Heffron
Your Adoption Guidebook, Deanna Kahler

Suggested Reading for Children

ABC, Adoption & Me: A Multicultural Picture Book Gayle H. Swift with Casey A. Swift

All Bears Need Love, Tanya Valentine

A Mother for Choco, Keiko Kasza

Billy Bramble and the Great Big Cook Off, Sally Donovan

Forever Fingerprints, Sherrie Eldridge

How I Was Adopted, Joanna Cole

In Our Mother's House, Patricia Polacco

Jazzy's Quest: Adopted and Amazing, Carrie Goldman and Juliet C. Bond LCSW

Little Branch Gets Adopted, Sherrie Eldridge

Motherbridge of Love, anonymous

A Place in My Heart, Mary Grossnickle.

Rosie's Family: An Adoption Story, Lori Rosove,

Star of the Week, Darlene Friedman

Tell Me Again about the Night I Was Born, Jamie Lee Curtis and Laura Cornell

Through Moon and Stars and Night Skies, Ann Turner

We're Adopted, So What, Gayle H. Swift and Casey A. Swift

We See the Moon, Carrie Kitze

Your Adoption Guidebook, Deanna Kahler

Bibliography

Association for Training on Trauma and Attachment in Children (ATTACH), Paperback, 2001. Hope for Healing: A Parent's Guide to Trauma and Attachment,

Augsberger, David, Caring Enough to Hear and Be Heard, Regal Books, 1982.

Ballard, Robert, Editor. Pieces of Me: Who do I Want to Be, EMK Press; First edition, 2009

Brodzinsky, David. Being Adopted: The Lifelong search for Self. Anchor Book, 1993

Christian, Diane Rene et al. Dear Wonderful You, Letters to Adopted & Fostered Youth (The AN-YA Project) Amazon Digital Services, 2014

Covey Stephen. The Seven Habits of Highly Effective People. Cambridge: Simon & Schuster; 1989

Cruver, Dan. The First Step in the Way Forward: A Response to David M. Smolin's "Of Orphans and Adoption. Journal of Christian Legal Thought, Spring 2013

Dennis, Laura, Editor Adopted Reality: A Memoir. Entourage Publishing, 2 Edition

Dennis, Laura, Adoption Therapy: Perspectives from Clients and Clinicians on Processing and Healing Post-Adoption Issues. Entourage Publishing, 2014

Eldridge, Sherrie. Twenty Things Adopted Kids Wish Their Adoptive Parents Knew. Delta, 1999

Eshelman, Lark, Ph.D. Becoming A Family: Promoting Healthy Attachments with Your Adopted Child, Taylor Trade Publishing, New York, 2003

Forbes, Heather T., LCSW. Dare to Love, Boulder: BCI, 2009

Gardner, Howard, Frames of Mind: The Theory of Multiple Intelligences, Basic Books; 3 edition, 2011

Grubb, Lynn et al. The Adoptee Survival Guide: Adoptees Share Their Wisdom and Tools,

CreateSpace Independent Publishing Platform

Heidegger, Martin, Being and Time, 1927

Holden, Lori and Crystal Hass. The Open-hearted Way to Open Adoption: Helping Your Child Grow up Whole. Lanham: Rowman and Littlefield Publishers. 2013

Johnston, Patricia Irwin. Adoption is a Family Affair. Jessica Kingsley Publishers. 2 editions, 2012

Joyce, Kathryn. The Child Catchers: Rescue, Trafficking, and the New Gospel of Adoption. New York: Public Affairs, 2013

Keefer, Betsey and Jayne Schooler, Telling the Truth to Your Adopted or Foster Child: Making Sense of the Past, Bergin & Garvey Trade; 1 edition, 2000

Lipton, Bruce. Ph.D.. The Biology of Belief. Original copyright @2005 by Bruce Lipton. Revised copright@2008 by Mountain of Love Productions. Hay House, Inc., Carlsbad, CA, New York City, London, Sydney, Johannesburg, Vancouver, Hong Kong, New Delhi

Naftziger, Katie. Parenting in the Eye of the Storm: The Adoptive Parent's Guide to Navigating the Teen Years, Jessica Kingsley Publishers, 2017

Nydam, Ronald J., Adoptees Come of Age, Louisville: Westminster John Knox Press, 1999

Pavao, Joyce Maguire. The Family of Adoption. Beacon Press, 2005

Purvis, Karen, Ph. D. and David R. Cross, Wendy Lyons. The Connected Child: Bring Hope and Healing to Your Adopted Child. Sunshine, McGraw Hill Education

Perry, M.D., Ph.D., Bruce D. The Boy Who Was Raised as a Dog: And Other Stories from a Child Psychiatrist's Notebook—What Traumatized Children Can Teach Us about Loss, Love, and Healing. Basic Books, 2017

Randolph, LMHC, Brooke, Editor. It's Not About You: Understanding Adoptee Search, Reunion, and Open Adoption, Mumbai: Entourage Publishing. 2017

Riley, Debbie, Beneath the Mask: Understanding Adopted Teens, C.A.S.E. Publications, 2005

Schooler, Jane et al. Wounded Children Healing Homes: How Traumatized Children Impact Adoptive and Foster Families, NavPress

Siegel, M.D., Dan and Tina Payne Bryson. The Whole-Brain Child: 12 Revolutionary Strategies to Nurture Your Child's Developing Mind. Bantam: 2012

Siegel, Daniel J. The Neurobiology of We –CD Set, Mind Your Brain, 2008

Smolin, David. Of Orphans and Adoption, Parents and the Poor, Exploitation and Rescue: A Scriptural and Theological Critique of the Evangelical Christian Adoption and Orphan Care Movement. Samford University. 2012

Solomon, Andrew. Far From the Tree: Parents, Children and the Search for Identity. Scribner. 2012

van der Kolk, M.D., Bessel. The Body Keeps Score: Brain, Mind and Body in the Healing of Trauma. New York: Viking. 2014

Verrier, Nancy. The Primal Wound: Understanding the Adopted Child. Louisville: Gateway Press, 1993

Wieirzbiki, Michael. Psychological Adjustment of Adoptees: A Meta-Analysis, Pages 447-454 | Published online: 07 Jun 2010, https://doi.org/10.1207/s15374424jccp2204_5

Ziegler, Ph.D., Dave, Traumatic Experience and the Brain: A Handbook for Understanding and Treating Those Traumatized as Children, Phoenix, Acacia Publishing

Index

"blank slates", 148
"Closed" adoptions, 54
"original belonging.", 63
"permanent children", 55
"public" life histories, 32
"shame" of an unplanned pregnancy, 113
"shoulding" on adoptees, 105
"sin" of unwed pregnancy, 113
"unsanitized" language, 157
"Unsanitized" Language, 150
abandonment, 83
Abraham, 84
accountability, 95
acknowledge missteps, 95
adopted
　as Children of God, 69
Adoptee
　as Big Winner, 113
Adoptee Rights Coalition, 53
adoptees
　as inferior, 38
Adoptees as broken, 36
adoption
　as a "joke", 39
　as a family experience, 121
　as a fresh start, 63
　as a life-long journey, 78
　as blessing, 30
　as declaration of faith, 35
　as emotional tug of war, 51
　as healing barrenness, 145
　as heroic, 29
　as rescue, 113
　as way to "visit", 69
　cause to win souls, 23
　in the media, 39
Adoption
　as Christian duty, 35
　as label, 38
　as positive solution, 118
　blends gain and losses, 34
Adoption History Project, 54
adoption industry, 26
adoption statistics, 154
Adoption statistics, 33
Adoption Takes Away the Pain of Infertility
　Adoption Takes Away the Pain of Infertility, 34
adoption training, 98
Adoption-attuned counsel, 107
Adoption-attuned response, 105
Adoption-attuned support, 41
adoption-attunement
　as Sixth element of Hierarchy of Needs, 50
Adoption-attunement, 12, 99

236

Adoption-attunement Elements, 12
Adoption-attunement Quotient, 11
adoption-competency, 118
adoption-connected needs, 125
adoptive-parent focused, 113
alliances, 70
amended birth certificate, 71
American Exceptionalism, 21
Ancestry.com, 49
AQ, 11, 53
as the abortion alternative
   as the abortion alternative, 39
attachment
   fear of, 111
Attachment, 235
attachment complexity, 112
Attachment Process, 109
attunement, 12
baby
   as evidence of sin, 31
baby as a sin, 92
Baby Scoop Era, 27, 30
backhanded compliments, 30
baptized, 32
bastardy, 31
Behavior
   as language of trauma, 111

Belief
   Adoption Is All Good, Yet Inferior, 28
Belief that America Knows Best and Is Best, 20
belonging, 42
   to both birth and adoptive families, 75
betrayal, 31
Bias, 26
biblical mandate, 66
Biological Psychiatry, 85
biological roots, 36
biology imposes the sentence, 85
birth certificates
   amended, 53
birth family's permanent role, 125
Birth grandparents, 116
birth heritage, 123
blessing
   of forgiveness, 95
BM, 158
Booker, Leslie, 102
both/and, 163
both/and dualities, 128
brokenness, 73
called to adopt, 132
Certificate of Adoption, 54
choose to parent, 114
chosen, 164
Christian adoption movement, 64
closed adoptions, 62
cock's crow, 32
command to adopt, 91

compassion, 98
compassionate witness., 105
Conflating Adoption and Abortion
  Conflating Adoption and Abortion, 39
control, 121
Covey, Steven, 122
crisis pregnancy, 114
Cruver, Dan, 68
Cultural Belief
  Adoptees Do Not Need To Know about Their Birth Families, 45
Cultural Practices, 36
cultural pressure, 155
Dan Cruver, 69, 73
Deuteronomy, 86
differences, respecting and nurturing, 126
Disclosure, 55
disruption, 162
Dissolution, 162
DNA, 25
Dr. Daniel Siegel, 11
Dr. Mark Umbreit, 16
Dr. Steven Porges, 11
dual heritages., 36
either/or perspective, 161
elements of AQ, 99
embodying radical presence, 102
Emotional Bank Account, 122
Emotional Intelligence, 100
Emotional Sanctuary, 106
empathy, 103
Epigenetics, 85
EQ, 100
erase first families, 77
fallen woman, 31
false equivalence, 90
family
  expanded definition, 72
first family, 63
forever family, 162
forgiveness, 95
FP365, 115
Fracture Accepted at the Font, 62
fractured parental relationships, 109
Full adoption, 64
fundraisers, 27
funeral, 60
Garden of — or how we should change to accommodate this diversity, 103
gaslighting, 47
Genealogical information
  as source of stability and roots, 50
genealogical roots, 123
General Biblical Themes, 82
General Cultural Beliefs, 19
Gethsemane, 105
Gethsemane experiences, 150
ghost status, 33

Gift from God, 165
God
  as broken-hearted, 77
God grieves, 142
God's opinion, 169
God's role in adoption, 143
God's will, 131, 135
Golden Rule, 128, 151
gossip, 119
grateful, 164
Great Commission Mandate, 67
grief and loss issues, 101
Grubb, Lynn, 115
healing trauma, 98
Hedeigger, Martin, 155
heirlooms, 126
heritage, 76
Hierarchy of Needs., 50
High AQ, 12
Holocaust, 98
Homilies, 108
honesty, 104
house of being, 155
identity, 36, 88
infertility, 127
Infertility, 34
influence
  influence understanding and interpretation of Scripture, 41
information
  belongs to child, 119
Innate Talents, 126
James 1:27, 90
Jesus, 119
Job, 135
John Winthrop, 21
joint scenario, 160
joke, 39
Joseph, 71, 136
Journal of Psychiatric Neuroscience and Therapeutics, 85
Joyce, Kathryn, 22
justifying adoption, 133
language
  transparency, 150
Language matters, 163
Language shapes experience, 147
Levine, Dr. Peter, 51
love as motive for relinquishment, 164
lucky, 164
Luke 15: 11-32, 89
Mark 8:29, 88
Maslow, Abraham, 49
Maté, Dr. Gabor, 85, 98
Matthew 5:-16, 101
Mementos, 125
metaphor, 148
money, 46
Money as a complicating factor, 160
Moses, 82
mother/child relationship, 83
Multiple Intelligences, 11
Nancy Verrier, 28
Normalization of Fracture, 60
Nydam, Ronald, 52
OBCs, 56
open adoption
  in the absence of direct interaction, 61

Open Adoption, 37, 232, 235
Open records, 56
original belonging, 74
Original Blessing, 73
Orphan and the Widow, 65
Orphan Train movement, 22
otherness, 38
PAL, 149
parental discouragement, 110
parenting blueprint
 blueprint, 118
parents
 resolve own grief and loss issues, 127
perfection, 37
platitudes, 153
playfulness, 122
Positive Adoption Language, 149
Positive intention, 167
power of words, 147
pre-birth matching, 159
prenatal stress, 85
President of Adoptees Rights Coalition, 115
presuppositions, 99
primal connection, 33
primal need for information about one's origins, 124
privacy boundaries, 120
privacy violations, 119
prodigal son, 89
Project of Salvation, 22
Psalm 127, 88
Psalm 139, 88

Psalms, 87
RAD, 112
rape, 87
Reactive Attachment Disorder, 112
real, 161
reconciliation, 95
Records
 unsealed, 56
registry of social service agencies, 114
rehoming, 162
relationship building, 122
relinquishment
 as act of love, 67
Relinquishment, 32
rescue, 26
resisting attachment, 110
respectful language, 158
Restorative dialogue, 17
right to exist, 45
safety, 143
sanitizing language, 30
Saving Our Sisters, 115
Schooler, Jane, 111
Scriptural Interpretation
 Supported the fracture of amilies, 59
Scripture
 as message of exclusion, 81
sealed records, 32, 52
Sealed records
 as anachronism, 53
searching, 47
Secrecy, 32
Secrets, 51
self-worth, 45
sermon, 77, 86

Seward Longfellow Restorative Justice Partnership, 16
shame, 32
 of infertility, 29
Shame, 51
Share knowledge, 100
sharing information, 119
Shroyer, Danielle, 73
Siegel, Dan, 12
silence, 47, 74
sins of the father, 84
Smolin, David, 64
social networks, 56
Solomon, 56, 84
spectrum of connection, 37
spiritual adoption, 69
 equivalence to legal adoption, 72
stand by women facing unplanned pregnancy, 114
stay awake to suffering, 103
Stephen Kinzer, 21
stigma of childlessness, 113
substance abuse, 48
suicidal, 90
suicide, 48
television, 50
Ten Commandments, 52
The Child Catchers, 22, 108
The Parable of the Lost Son, 89
The Primal Wound, 28
toxic phrases, 157
transgenerational trauma, 85
trauma, 23
Trauma, 85, 102, 234, 235
truth, 51
Truth, 52
unadopted, 36
undivided loyalty, 125
ungrateful, 41, 102
unmarried, 141
unmarried mothers, 87
unredacted records, 53
unsolicited advice, 30, 40
unvarnished truth, 151
validate adoptee pain, 144
Validate the Full Spectrum of Adoption Experience, 106
We Deserve the Family of Our Dreams
 We Deserve the Family of Our Dreams, 23
What Faith Communities Can Do, 95
what ifs, 49
What would Jesus do?, 91
Whitewashing grief and loss, 103
witness, 77
witnesses, 114
witnesses to suffering, 103
zero-sum g, 124
Ziegler, Ph.D., Dave, 112

About the Authors

Sally Ankerfelt
Co-Founder of GIFT Family Services, LLC, and a certified coach has over 19 years of personal adoption experience. She holds a Certificate in Trauma Studies from the University of Minnesota which informs her work as a coach. In addition, Sally has worked with individuals and families for over 26 years as an ordained Lutheran pastor.

Gayle H. Swift
Co-Founder of GIFT Family Services, LLC and a certified coach, adoptive parent, Adoptee Rights activist, and an award-winning author Gayle uses her love of writing to serve her goal of supporting adoptees and their families.

Titles Available for children

Multi-award-winning book" Touches on many aspects of adoption that could be difficult to talk about, but not in a threatening or forceful way. It can be used over and over again as children grow."—**Adoptive Families Magazine**, ages 5-10

Authored by the same award-winning mother-daughter duo, who wrote *ABC, Adoption & Me,* this book tackles many challenging issues with which young adoptees must cope. Written from the perspective of five teen girls. Available, July 2019   Ages 10-15

"This is a treasure and will help so many families. I love this book so much. I wish I'd had it when my kids were younger.)—Lori Holden, author ***The Open-hearted Way to Open Adoption: Helping Your Child Grow Up Whole***

"My hope is that prospective adoptive parents will buy and read this book before they become parents. Good adoptive parenting requires you to first seek to understand your child's perspective. Owning this book is a good first step."—Lynn Grubb, adoptee and kinship adoptive parent, editor and creator of ***The Adoptee Survival Guide.***

If you find value in these books, please consider posting a review on Amazon, Facebook, Twitter, etc. Tell your friends about them as well. This will help others find these books. Thank you for joining our effort to support adoptees and the families who love them.

Testimonials

"This book opens people of faith to a different perspective than what you would normally hear in mainstream media, your church and your community about adoption. Share it with your pastor, your congregation, and other people of faith." —Lynn Grubb, Adoptee, Kinship Adoptive Parent. Editor, ***The Adoptee Survival Guide***

"Talking with co-author, Sally, was cathartic. I have been grappling with how faith intersects with cultural identity and family dynamics. Talking about my journey was healing and thought-provoking. Sharing my storying and reading a book that uses real voices, real words, and real experiences validated my own experience. This book elevated my faith. It is a rare find." —Lolita, fosteree, child welfare professional

www.ingramcontent.com/pod-product-compliance
Lightning Source LLC
Chambersburg PA
CBHW071154070526
44584CB00019B/2787